Twentieth Century Composers

VOLUME III

Britain, Scandinavia and The Netherlands

Twentieth Century Composers

Edited by
Nicolas Nabokov and Anna Kallin

Twentieth Century Composers

VOLUME III

Britain, Scandinavia and The Netherlands

Humphrey Searle
and Robert Layton

Holt, Rinehart and Winston
New York Chicago San Francisco

Library of Congress Catalog Card Number: 75-155529

First published in the United States in 1973.

ISBN: 0-03-003381-0

Printed in Great Britain

Contents

Acknowledgments

I would like to thank the Librarian of the Royal College of Music for the loan of books, Miss Viola Tunnard for her valuable assistance and my wife for her help in typing the manuscript.

H.S.

The authors and publishers wish to record their gratitude for permission received from owners, agents and photographers to reproduce the following list of illustrations (numbers refer to pictures): Sir Arthur Bliss 8; Imogen Holst 7; Lelia Goehr 21; Humphrey Searle 17; Mrs R. Vaughan-Williams 5, 6;

Bassano and Vandyk Studios 3; Camera Press 13, 18, 19, 22; Donemus, Amsterdam 25, 26, 27, 28; Foto Maria, Austria: Amsterdam 29; Nordisk Pressefoto 30, 32, 35 (and Institutet för Färgfoto Malmö), 36 (and Tage Nielsen), 37 (and AA Mortensen), 38, 39 (and Erik Holmberg), 40; I. Nousiainen 41; Popperfoto 9, 14; Radio Times Hulton Picture Library 1, 2, 11, 12, 15, 16, 23; Royal Norwegian Embassy 33 (and Billedsentralen, Oslo), 34; A. Sirot, Paris 31; Thomson Newspapers 4, 10, 24; John Vere Brown 20.

Illustrations

Introduction
Twentieth Century Makers of Music

BY NICOLAS NABOKOV

This is not history nor is it a chronicle although perforce it deals with chronology. It is rather an imaginary map of twentieth-century music. Like all maps it is divided into regions and these regions represent loose cultural entities determined in turn by ethnic and geographical cohesion.

All choices made by the authors of these volumes are personal ones. They express personal views, personal agonisms and antagonisms, personal tastes and judgments of value and of historical importance. But in so far as each author knows the musical life of his region each volume can be relied upon as being a fair albeit a personal description of what has happened to music in the region of his particular concern during the twentieth century.

The language used in these books is intentionally unencumbered by a *fatras* of technical terms. It is I believe accessible to the average reader and music lover. It will give him a more coherent and detailed picture of the 'state of music' – to use the title of a famous book – than if it were cluttered by technical terms and followed the chronological evolutionary paths of music history.

Do these books, these regional essays, concerned primarily with the most important composers of the twentieth century lack historical value? I do not think so. Precisely because the views expressed in them are personal and hence obviously partisan, they may be a refreshing contribution to music history.

For however imaginary or even arbitrary a cartographic division may appear to be, it deals with concrete facts and with a great variety of musical happenings.

The regional divisions are limited to Europe and America; the reason is obvious. First we do not deal with non-Western musical traditions, however valuable and ancient they may be; second until the middle of this century there were no significant contributions from non-European and non-American regions. I am well aware that since the second half of this century there have appeared a number of gifted composers in Japan and elsewhere. Still all valuable twentieth-century music has so far been composed in Europe and America. New discoveries in musical language, stylistic changes, technical innovations, all of them stem from here and were later adopted or copied elsewhere.

But when does this century start? Surely not in 1900; datelines are arbitrary landmarks. They rarely coincide with a change of heart and mind or indicate the rise of a new style or of a new technique. The case of the Florentine musical Renaissance, or of Monteverdi's first operas in Venice at the turn of the seventeenth century, are convenient exceptions. Usually new centuries begin or end long before or after their datelines.

Yet no one will deny that there is such a thing as *l'esprit du siècle.* When we say 'This is an eighteenth-century Italian opera,' or 'This is seventeenth-century Spanish court music,' we know what we mean, and anyone acquainted with music history will understand what is being said. *L'esprit du siècle* is something intangible and yet concrete; it has little to do with dates or date-lines. Sometimes it ripens late in the century (*vide* Mozart); sometimes it overlaps two centuries (*Vide* Haydn). J. S. Bach and Handel wrote their grandiose works in the first half of the eighteenth century, but does their work represent the spirit of the *siècle des lumières*? Certainly not. Both Bach and Handel however extraordinary their achievements stand at the end, at the completion of a long stylistic evolution and of a historical period, whereas their contemporary Domenico Scarlatti for instance (all three were born in 1685) especially in his last, Spanish period points the way into the future and is far more daring and experimental than the two grand Germans.

Century crossings are like traffic crossings. Lights are announced in advance and arrows point in different directions; forward, backward, and sideways. In the case of twentieth-century music the greenest of all lights, whose arrow points straight into the future, is of course Claude Debussy. To a minor extent this is true of Alexander Scriabin, despite the Chopinesque and Lisztian gloss that covers so much of his early music.

Rimsky-Korsakov's arrow points sideways. He belongs only in part to our century and is of course one of its outstanding pedagogues and masters of orchestration. Finland's Sibelius, that hypertrophic symphonic bard so dear to Anglo-Saxon audiences of the 1930s, is the opposite of an innovator. Whether good or bad his music does not belong to our century's concerns and worries. Like the music of other symphony composers it represents the continuation of the nineteenth century in the midst of the twentieth. His light is red; the arrow points backward.

But what then is the *esprit* of our century? What does it consist of; what are its distinguishing signs? Can it be described, circumscribed, evaluated? Of course it can but only in a general, hazy way. Partly because it is not yet quite 'fulfilled,' partly because we ourselves are in the midst of it and lack perspective to look at it objectively.

One of our century's distinguishing features is fairly obvious – the quickening pace of change, the extraordinary profusion of experimentation, and (what could have been foreseen since Wagner) the concomitant breakdown of so-called 'academic' rules and traditions. Rarely before in the short history of Western music has there been such an *accélération de l'histoire* to use the title of a famous essay by the French historian Daniel Halévy.

Another early discernible aspect of this century's musical production is its variety. Dozens of different aesthetic and technical trends (often contradictory) coexist peacefully (or not) and fill the publishing houses and blue-printing presses, or gather dust on conductors' shelves and piano-tops. Perhaps a more particular, sociological distinguishing mark of this century's music is its increasing urbanization. Although rural elements, materials, and folkloristic memories still linger in it, they are purely reflective. In one way or another all of twentieth-century music has served urban needs and reflected urban life and urban outlooks. There has been little *plein-air* stuff produced by the composers of this century. Our musical trouts do not hop around in brooks and mountain streams; they are flown in by airplane and served blue or sautéed in megalopolitan restaurants. As for our present-day advanced music it is recorded and fractured on tape, seasoned and peppered by electronic sound, and salted by computers. All of it addresses itself to city dwellers, not to rural folk.

With this general trend towards urbanization goes a constant search, a perpetual metamorphosis of the musical language. The fundamental change is brought about by the discovery of a new compositional technique devised in Vienna at the beginning of this century. It had of course been foreshadowed by earlier developments but never stated as a complete logical method for musical composition. It is based on atonality and uses as its structural principle *series* constructed out of the autonomous, rootless, and equi-valid twelve tones of the chromatic scale. It discards once and forever the distinction between consonance and dissonance.

Quite a number of composers have accepted this technique as soon as it was stated; others have staunchly rejected it; others again have gone further and have experimented with musical structures made of smaller particles than semitones. Curiously enough the Latin and the Slavic worlds remained impervious to the twelve-tone serial technique for a very long time. Only after World War II did serialism penetrate the French and Italian preserves where it has now been adopted by young composers and by a few older ones as part of an inevitable evolution of music.

Russia alone remains officially impervious to the serial technique, though unofficially it is I am told being used by many composers of the younger generation. Nowadays serial technique has penetrated other elements of the musical language such as metrical divisions, rhythm, dynamics, intensity of sound, and timbre. All of them undergo serial treatments in the works of some of the most able advanced composers.

Another important innovation that enriched the language of twentieth-century music and enhanced its vocabulary is due to the discovery of electronic sound. The possibility of producing electronic sound has been known for quite some time, but the first usable instrument was built in 1920 by a Russian engineer (and amateur cellist) Lev Teremin. I remember seeing it and experimenting with it under Teremin's guidance in the 1920s. It looked like a movable antenna and could produce a great variety of sounds. What Teremin liked best about it – and I least – was its ability to imitate the sound of a cello. 'You don't need to use your clumsy fingers on a string anymore,' he would say. In 1928 Maurice Martenot presented his far more perfected electronic instrument to the Parisian public. It is endowed with a keyboard, has been widely used by composers, and is a mainstay of symphony orchestras.

But the use of integral electronic sound for musical composition has come about only after World War II and paralleled a general advance in electronics. In the late 1940s and early 1950s serviceable electronic studios devised especially for musical composition started to mushroom first in Europe, then in America, and in Japan. With this came at once a sizeable production of purely electronic or partly electronic music. By now it is firmly rooted in our century's music as one of its important branches.

The last technical innovation and the latest one chronologically is the use of computers for musical composition. So far only a few composers have experimented successfully with it. But electronics and the computer might, I believe, realize the dream of a few early pioneers of this century who had hoped that '*all* sounds should be put at the disposal of composers.' Now this hope is a reality. It is difficult to foresee what it will do to the art of music. It may of course change its nature as an art. It may make music a branch of technology or something belonging to the world of mathematics, physics, symbolic logic, and games of chance.

Chance (aleatoric) improvisation or invention within a given framework (as in Indian music) or without it, games with sound structures are now widely used by far-out composers all over the world. Games and 'gaming' have long been missing in music; yet once upon a time in the fifteenth and sixteenth centuries they were an essential part of musical composition.

Because of mass communication music in our century has long ceased to be the privileged pleasure of an educated elite and has become a consumers' commodity. It can now be pumped through any hole, at any time, into any space, like air into flat tyres. It is unavoidably consumed by millions of people who do not even notice what they are consuming.

The Northern Realm

This is the third volume of the anthological series of Twentieth Century Composers. It is high time that a book like this came out in print and, so to speak, put the record straight.

But what record one may ask? The answer is given by the book itself, by its complexity, by the variety of aesthetic trends it discusses and with which it deals, and also in the fullness and richness of the musical scene it describes. The average inhabitant of continental Europe and to a large extent of America, has not the slightest idea about any of it.

'Das Land ohne Musik', a nineteenth-century slogan tagged to anything from England by the then so powerful Germans, made a deep and lasting dent in the psychological attitude of the average continental European towards the music of the Northern Realm whether it be English or Scandinavian or Dutch. Coming at a time when British musical life was at a very low ebb it created a climate in which it was easy to believe that anything that did not take place in Paris, or Vienna, or Berlin, or at La Scala or, from the beginning of the century, in St Petersburg was co-ipso peripheral to the destinies of The Art of Music. The *'vital centres'* of the Continent took care of 'innovation' (when needed), of 'evolution' (when unavoidable), or 'revolutions' (when upon them) – the periphery's task was to follow it all as best it could, considering, of course, that it never could match in quality and validity what was being produced by the *'vital centres'*.

This negative attitude towards musical production across the channel, or North and West of the Kiel Canal reminds one ironically of the colonial attitude of nineteenth century blimps guarding the European glories in India, Burma or elsewhere. In the eyes of the French, and the Germans, certainly of the Russians not to mention the Americans, Britain and its music was to all intents and purposes a musical colony of Europe and, to boot, a colony of little interest and no consequence.

Mr Searle's and Mr Layton's volume proves that nothing was the way one thought it had been. That, for instance, one of the best serial composers of all time was neither Viennese, nor French, nor German, but a grand British lady; that one of the best symphonists of this century, by far superior to his German, Soviet or French counterparts was British, and that the tightest most poignant Chamber opera scores were produced by an Englishman, and not by a Russian, or German, or Frenchman, or Italian or even an American. And this same comparison is, I am sure, valid for quite a large part of the Scandinavian musical production so ably dealt with by Mr Layton.

All I can say while writing these lines in an *island* called Paris, is 'Music Ho!'. Let us blast the Music of the Northern Realm into the ears and the unknowing minds of the Islanders, the Europeans. Maybe one day they will awaken to the facts so simply and carefully recalled in this book.

I The last romantics - Elgar and Delius

Until the late nineteenth century there was little concern in England with producing music of a distinctively national character; composers were, in most cases, able craftsmen catering for the tastes of a cosmopolitan ruling class. It was amateur choral societies located through the country that at last began to demand new music bearing a direct relationship to their activities and attitudes; Hubert Parry and Charles Villiers Stanford, the leaders of this movement, were gentlemen-composers who did much to set English music in the context of a general notion of English culture. Only a few years later came Edward Elgar who, coinciding perfectly with the altered climate, arose as a major composer in a new English tradition despite the fact that he did not consciously involve himself with the currents of his time.

Hubert Parry (1848–1918) came from a wealthy West Country family, and was educated at Eton and Oxford. He was a prolific composer from his Eton days, and when the Royal College of Music was opened in 1883 he joined its staff, becoming its director eleven years later. He was the first to insist on linking music with general artistic culture, and caused something of a sensation when he chose a text from Shelley's *Prometheus Unbound* for a cantata for the Gloucester Festival of 1880. Most of his works were choral, but he also wrote five symphonies and a piano concerto. His music shows German influences, particularly those of Bach and Brahms, almost throughout. If, apart from *Blest Pair of Sirens* (1887) little is performed today, it nevertheless represents a standard higher than anything composed in England earlier in the nineteenth century.

The Irishman Charles Villiers Stanford (1852–1924) was educated in Dublin and later at Cambridge. Like Parry, he joined the staff of the Royal College of Music; he was also Professor of Music at Cambridge. In his large catalogue of works are choral compositions such as the *Stabat Mater* and the *Requiem,* several operas (which were performed in Germany before being heard in England), symphonies and some Irish rhapsodies. His music contains some elements derived from Irish folk-song, but not to the extent which was to be typical of Vaughan Williams and the folk-song school of a later generation. Although always competently written, his music lacks originality, and not much of it is performed today. As a teacher, however, he had a very great influence.

Edward Elgar was born at Broadheath, Worcester on 2 June 1857, and was self-taught. Students of horoscopes may find it significant that he was born under the sign of Gemini; throughout his life a dual personality was very much in evidence. Behind the public image of the tall, much decorated gentleman of military appearance there hid a shy, uneasy man who, for the last fourteen years of his life, was desperately lonely. Such a duality can often be seen within one and the same work; in both the *Cockaigne Overture* and the first symphony, for instance, passages of military brilliance co-exist with others of lyrical nostalgia. Elgar's letters, with their curious mixture of banter and chaff, reveal his need to mask his true feelings, often very bitter ones.

Although he was brought up in an atmosphere of music, it was not obvious that he would one day emerge as a major composer. His father served for a short time as assistant in a music shop in London, and in his early forties came to Worcester, where he became organist of St George's Catholic Church, as well as starting a music shop in the town. A better musician than businessman, he played the violin in the Three Choirs Festival in Worcester and also worked as a piano tuner (one of his idiosyncracies being to arrive at his clients' houses on a thoroughbred horse). His business was not a great success, largely because he was never able to attend to the necessary book-keeping.

Elgar's musical interests were encouraged from an early age by lessons in violin and organ playing and by the music in his father's shop. His self-tutoring included the viola, cello and later the bassoon. While still at school he deputized for his father as organist at St George's, and was able to study the tradition of Anglican church music at Worcester Cathedral, where the organist, Mr Done, a staunch conservative loathing the music of Schumann as being far too modern, introduced him to the works of the older English church composers as well as to Corelli, Haydn and Handel. He made his earliest attempts at composition when he was fifteen. By the time he was a year older, he took his place among the violins at the concert of the Worcester Glee Club, as well as playing the bassoon in a wind quintet for which he wrote a number of pieces.

Thus at an early age he was a very practical all-round musician, but in order to help with the family finances he took a job in a solicitor's office when he was fifteen. Here he was given only menial duties, and a year later he announced his intention of helping his father in the music shop, undertaking the book-keeping. He even saved enough money to enable him to go to London to take some violin lessons from Adolf Pollitzer, a pupil of Boehm, who had been Joachim's teacher. Recognizing Elgar's gifts as a violinist, Pollitzer tried to persuade him to take up the instrument as a career, but after careful consideration Elgar rejected the idea and returned to Worcester. There he played in the orchestra for the Three Choirs Festivals and, more important, in 1877 he was appointed bandmaster of the Worcester County Lunatic

Asylum. The band consisted of two cornets, euphonium, bombardon, flute, clarinet, two violins, double bass and piano. For this curious combination Elgar composed a number of quadrilles at the request of the governors of the asylum. The significance of this appointment was that it gave him experience in conducting, and shortly afterwards he was appointed pianist and conductor of the Worcester Glee Club as well. (Throughout his life he remained an admirable conductor of his own works, as may be judged from the recordings he made in his last years.)

But although these years were vital to his craftsmanship and later successes, for the moment Elgar remained a provincial musician. He did some teaching, wrote liturgical music for Catholic services at St George's, and studied and played organ music. (At this time an incident took place which may have contributed to Elgar's later attitude of withdrawal from life. An anthem with orchestra had been written by a church musician of moderate talent; at rehearsal, it was found to be so badly scored that Elgar was asked to rescore it. He greatly improved the work, but received no acknowledgement at the performance. It was this kind of incident that led him to say in later life that he preferred dogs to human beings as companions.)

Having managed to save some money, Elgar was able to fulfil a long-standing ambition by spending a three-week holiday in Leipzig, a city which was regarded as a Mecca by the English musicians of that day. Elgar had no wish to study abroad, but he did want to hear the famous Gewandhaus orchestra. Home in Worcester once again, he was appointed conductor of the Amateur Instrumental Society, and also succeeded his father as organist of St George's Church. All this left him little time for composition.

It is possible that Elgar would have remained a local musician all his life had he not in 1886 met Caroline Alice Roberts. Sharing a passion for literature and music, they soon became close friends. She was his pupil, taking piano lessons from him. On the face of it, it seemed an unsuitable match. Not only was she eight years his senior, but she was the daughter of Major General Sir Henry Roberts, a distinguished and wealthy man. As a relatively poor musician, the son of a shopkeeper and a Roman Catholic, Elgar was decidedly not in her class, and accordingly the match met with strong opposition from her family. Objections notwithstanding, they were married on 9 May 1889 at Brompton Oratory; Alice was forty and Elgar was then thirty-two.

As a wedding present, Father Knight of St George's, Worcester gave Elgar a copy of Newman's poem, *The Dream of Gerontius.* In a sense this gift was symbolic, for it presaged the period of Elgar's greatest creativity. But of far greater importance was the influence of his wife on the composer: the immediate effect of Elgar's marriage was to turn him from a provincial into a national musician.

The pair set up home in London where Elgar lived by teaching, but was able to find more time to compose; a year after his marriage his overture *Froissart* was accepted for performance at the Three Choirs Festival in Worcester. In London he was able to hear a wide range of classical music for the first time since his short stay in Leipzig. Stimulating though London was to a musician, as a composer Elgar made little headway at first. He was able to sell some salon pieces, such as the famous *Salut d'Amour,* to publishers for small sums; he was promised some try-outs at orchestral rehearsals, but these did not come about. In 1891, in a mood of depression, Elgar and his wife returned to Malvern: it was there that Elgar's creative talents at last began to flower. The cantatas *The Black Knight, King Olaf, The Banner of St George* and *Caractacus* and the oratorio *The Light of Life* all belong to this period.

The only work of this period to survive into the modern repertoire is the *Serenade for Strings,* a charming piece which shows the lyrical and nostalgic side of Elgar's nature. An important step came when he was asked to write a work for the Leeds Festival in 1898: *Caractacus,* a cantata based on the fate of the king of Britain during the Roman occupation, was the response, and it was a great success. Much encouraged, Elgar embarked on a large-scale work which was to bring him both national and international fame, the *Enigma Variations*. The composer dedicated the work 'to my friends pictured within' and it is in fact a series of portraits of the composer's friends, culminating in one of the composer himself. Though based on a single theme, the variations differ considerably in character, being lyrical, nostalgic, brilliant and ferocious by turns; one of them even represents the subject's dog instead of his master. Each variation is concisely written and makes its mark immediately, and for this reason, combined with the mastery of the orchestral writing, the work has remained in the repertory for the last seventy years. The 'enigma' which gave the work its title is supposed to be a counter-theme which 'goes with' the main theme, but Elgar refused to give an explanation of it, adding that its 'dark saying' must be left unguessed.*

The fame which Elgar attained aroused some jealousy on the part of his fellow composers, particularly Stanford, who wrote in *The Oxford History of Music*: 'English music has not yet shown signs of an exhausted and moribund fertility by taking refuge from sheer lack of ideas in the over-elaboration of detail at the cost of purity of design'. This was clearly a hit at Elgar, who, apart from having no academic training, was known to admire such un-English composers as Meyerbeer, Berlioz, Goldmark, and later Busoni.

However, Elgar, undeterred, continued to compose, and *The Dream of Gerontius* was commissioned for the Birmingham Festival of 1900; it was a work he had long been considering. Although Hans Richter, who had introduced the *Enigma Variations* to the world, again conducted, the première was a failure. Apparently the chorus was largely to blame, for the soloists were first rate. When Elgar, who had agreed to supervise the final rehearsal, heard the choral

*A possible explanation is given by Ian Parrott in his *Elgar* (Dent, 1971).

singing, he was shocked. At his instigation there was a further rehearsal on the day before the performance; it lasted for six hours, at the end of which everyone was exhausted – no wonder the performance itself was something of a fiasco. To their credit, there were some critics who discerned the work's merits. Some musicians, too, were much impressed; not so Stanford, who conmented: 'It stinks of incense'. To this day opinions are divided, as indeed they are over many of Elgar's major works; but in the case of *Gerontius* the strong Catholic flavour is at least partially responsible. The Birmingham misrepresentation of the composition could well have resulted in its neglect for many years to come, but August Jaeger, a member of the publishing house of Novello and a close friend of Elgar, had invited Professor Julius Buths of Düsseldorf to the Birmingham performance. Buths was immensely impressed and immediately arranged to give a performance of *Gerontius* at Düsseldorf, and the result vindicated the work. On that occasion Richard Strauss toasted Elgar in these words: 'I raise my glass to the welfare and success of the first English progressivist, Maestro Edward Elgar'. As one of the most celebrated composers of the day, Strauss's acknowledgement of and belief in Elgar's genius were noted by those who had dismissed *Gerontius* in England; they reversed their judgements. *Gerontius* is a long work, and though one of Elgar's most heart-felt compositions, it shows some unevennesses. The style is reminiscent of *Parsifal* here and there, though Elgar speaks with an individual voice through much of the work. It is intensely dramatic in places, such as Gerontius' *Sanctus fortis* and the great chorus *Praise to the Holiest in the height*. It is a landmark in the history of British oratorio, and like *Enigma* has held its place in the repertory ever since.

Elgar was now well into his finest period of creation. In 1901 the *Cockaigne Overture* was given its first performance in London. The composer described the piece to Richter as 'nothing deep or melancholy but intended to be honest, healthy, humorous and strong, but not vulgar'. To the same year belonged the first two *Pomp and Circumstance* marches. Elgar has often been criticised for writing pieces of this kind, but they represent one side of his dual nature, and of their kind are extremely good. They may be vulgar, but at least they are full-blooded, which is more than can be said for the pallid creations of many of Elgar's contemporaries. He did not yet hold the post of Master of the King's Musick, but he was asked to write the official ode in honour of Edward VII's coronation. Two years later he was knighted.

Although honoured at home and well known in Germany and America, where *Gerontius* was also performed, Elgar lacked financial security, and because of this he took the post of Professor of Music at Birmingham University in 1905. He told his friends he had no more desire to write music. Instead, most of his time was taken up by walking, cycling, kite-flying, chemistry and solving cryptograms.

However, his creativity was far from exhausted. In 1907–8 he at last began work on the symphony he had long been contemplating. It was performed at Manchester under Richter on 3 December 1908, and in the first year of its life it had no less than a hundred performances. On 10 November 1910 the *Violin Concerto* was first produced at the Queen's Hall, London, with the composer conducting. The soloist was the Austrian Fritz Kreisler, the most famous violinist of his day, and the work has since been played by most of the greatest violinists in the world. Shortly before his death Elgar himself made a recording of it with the sixteen-year-old Yehudi Menuhin. The concerto is a long and somewhat wayward work: it is effectively written for both the soloist and the orchestra, but the predominant feeling is of lyrical nostalgia rather than brilliance, in spite of many exciting passages of a more forceful nature. A feature of the finale is an extended cadenza for the soloist in which the strings of the orchestra accompany him with soft 'thrummed' chords marked 'pizzicato tremolando'.

Then came the second symphony; less brilliant and flamboyant than the first, it puzzled some of the composer's friends, but both symphonies have achieved a firm place in the modern repertoire.

Both the *Violin Concerto* and the *Symphony No. 2* are prefaced by quotations or mottoes; the one on the concerto reads in Spanish: *Aqui esta encerrada el alma de* . . . (*Here is enshrined the soul of* . . .). It has been discovered that the missing name was that of an American lady who was a close friend of the Elgars. On the *Symphony No. 2* are some words from Shelley: 'Rarely, rarely comest thou, Spirit of Delight!'

The last orchestral work of this period was the symphonic poem *Falstaff*. Many admirers of Elgar consider this to be one of his greatest works, though others have found it difficult to understand without a knowledge of the detailed programme which the composer himself wrote. *Falstaff* is a portrait of the fat knight as seen in Shakespeare's Henry plays rather than in *The Merry Wives of Windsor,* and in order to follow the music it is necessary to have a fairly detailed knowledge of these plays. There are themes representing the different characters, as in Strauss's symphonic poems, but the music is very much conditioned by the sequence of events in these plays and so the musical form does not really become evident as such – unlike the rondo form of *Till Eulenspiegel* and the variation form of *Don Quixote.* So that in spite of some fine dramatic and lyrical music and two delightful self-contained interludes *Falstaff* has never really succeeded as a piece of symphonic music in its own right. But it is in many ways an interesting work, and makes a worthy ending to a creative period which also includes the well-known *Introduction and Allegro* for string orchestra (1904).

The First World War marked a new stage in Elgar's career. He was now regarded as the unofficial Composer Laureate of England, so it was natural that he should produce a number of works inspired by the war. These are not much more than occasional pieces; more important are the choral works which together make up *The Spirit of England,* settings of poems by Laurence Binyon. The works which mark his last important creative period are the *Violin Sonata, String Quartet* and *Piano Quintet,* all completed in 1918, as well as the *Cello Concerto* of the following year. In these works a new Elgar can be discerned: the old flamboyance has gone, and they breathe a quiet, nostalgic, almost chastened atmosphere. The *Cello Concerto,* in contrast with the luxuriant length of the *Violin Concerto,* is short and concise and gives an impression almost of world-weariness, although flashes of humour and many passages of great lyrical beauty occur, especially in the slow movement and towards the end of the work. It has been played by Casals, Feuermann, Fournier and Tortelier, as well as by all British cellists.

In 1920 Lady Elgar died. Elgar never recovered from the loss; writing to his friend, the violinist W. H. Reed, he says: 'I am not very well and have lost all interest in life and I fear that nothing will ever revive it – the wrench was too severe'. Elgar returned to the West Country, where he lived to the end of his life.

In 1924 he was asked to contribute some incidental music to the Empire Exhibition at Wembley. He found the arrangements for this last event extremely trying and wrote to a friend:

> I have been at Wembley and am overwhelmed with etiquette and red tape. The Wembley affair will be a mixture; there were some ludicrous suggestions . . . But everything seems so hopelessly and irredeemably *vulgar* at Court . . . I was standing alone (criticising) in the middle of the enormous stadium, all the ridiculous Court programme, soldiers, . . . etc.; seventeen thousand men hammering, loudspeakers, amplifiers, four aeroplanes circling over etc., etc., all mechanical and horrible, no soul and no romance and no imagination.

Elgar fled from this atmosphere back to the West Country. Shortly afterwards he was appointed Master of the

King's Musick. In these years he began a close friendship with Bernard Shaw, and the correspondence between them showed how much they admired each other's work. He wrote only a few more works; these include the *Severn Suite* for brass band of 1930 and the *Nursery Suite* of 1931 for the Princesses Elizabeth and Margaret.

At the age of seventy-six he flew to Paris to conduct the *Violin Concerto*; on his way back to England he visited Delius, who at the time was far from well. On the whole his last years were spent quietly at his house near Worcester, exercising his dogs, reading and listening to music, and pursuing his hobbies of crossword puzzles – he preferred the Torquemada variety – heraldry and horse-racing. He died on 23 February 1934.

Frederick Delius was a man of very different character. He was born at Bradford, Yorkshire on 29 January 1862; his family on both sides were Germans from Westphalia who had settled in Bradford and worked in the wool trade. Delius always maintained that his family was of Dutch origin, which may have been true. Frederick was the fourth of twelve children; his father was the typical Prussian domestic tyrant, and his mother, although less severe, was nonetheless so uninterested in Delius's progress in later years that she never heard a note of his music. His father was interested in music to some extent, and a certain number of visiting artists, including celebrities such as Joachim and Piatti, occasionally came to make music at the Delius home. Delius soon learnt to play the violin and piano. Outdoor pursuits such as riding, walking and playing cricket also attracted him, and he adored travelling circuses, especially the bareback riders and the trapeze artists.

He received his first education at Bradford Grammar School and then attended the International College at Isleworth, near London, where he was to learn the rudiments of office life. He remained there for three years. During the time of his business studies he did not neglect his musical interests. At the beginning of 1881 he entered the family business, apparently with no great reluctance. He was sent to Chemnitz in Saxony, not far from both Leipzig and Dresden, where he was able to hear a great deal of music, and managed to study the violin. The great event of this period was his introduction to Wagner's *Meistersinger*. However news soon reached his parents that he was neglecting the family business, and he was recalled to Bradford.

This was a pattern that was to be repeated many times before both Delius and his family tired of it. In June 1882 his father was persuaded to send him to Sweden to do business for the wool trade. After a few weeks of work for the firm, Delius went to Stockholm, then to the Swedish countryside, and later to the Norwegian mountains and fjords. This country with its high and lonely regions appealed greatly to him and he was later to write many works inspired by it. Again he was summoned back to face the wrath of his father, who this time sent him to Saint-Étienne in France, a town concerned only with the buying and selling of wool. Delius soon tired of it; to escape he went to Monte Carlo, where he staked all his money on the roulette tables – and won. His luck enabled him to spend several weeks on the Riviera, during which he attended concerts and operas and took further violin lessons, before being hauled back to England yet again, via Saint-Étienne. There followed a second visit to Norway; by now, having learnt a certain amount of Norwegian, he was able to follow Ibsen's plays in the theatre.

A short stint at the family office in Manchester further strengthened the feeling that he was not suited to a commercial career. An uncle of his in Paris urged Delius to inquire whether, even though the wool trade was obviously not his forte, there was no other form of commerce to which he might prove better suited. There appeared to be commercial possibilities in growing oranges in the north-eastern part of Florida, and in March 1884 Delius and a companion sailed to Florida, to a property at Solano Grove. He was twenty-two.

The tropical profusion of his surroundings excited him as much as the Norwegian mountains had. For the first time he heard the music of the Negroes. One day, in the nearby town of Jacksonville, he happened to meet a musician from New York in a music shop. This was Thomas F. Ward, organist of a Jesuit church in Brooklyn. Upon returning to Solano Grove, Delius found that his business companion had disappeared. He invited Ward to stay with him, which he did for some months, during which time Ward taught him counterpoint and fugue. Delius later said this was the only instruction he ever had.

Delius was as little interested in oranges as in work and wanted to go to Leipzig to study, but being entirely dependent on his father for money, he could not simply leave Solano. By good chance his elder brother, who had been sheep-farming in New Zealand, appeared to see if there was any work on the estate for himself. Delius promptly put him in charge and left, not for Leipzig, but for Jacksonville, where early in 1885 he set himself up as a music teacher. Soon after he took a teaching position in Danville, Virginia, where 'Professor Delius' was appointed music teacher at a finishing school for Baptist Young Ladies.

Delius became financially successful in Danville, remaining there till the spring of 1886, when he set off for New York. Meanwhile, his brother had left Solano Grove and disappeared into the unknown. When their father decided to get Frederick back to Europe he had to trace him through a private enquiry agent. Perhaps because music had brought Frederick financial success, he overcame his objections to music as a career for his son, and became willing for him to study at the Leipzig Conservatoire. He made only one condition – that after Leipzig Delius should return to the United States and continue his money-making there.

In the last quarter of the nineteenth century Leipzig was the centre of the musical world. Apart from the eminent teachers at the Conservatorium it possessed a first class opera which performed Wagner's works, often with Nikisch as guest conductor, as well as the famous Gewandhaus orchestra. Delius had written a few songs and piano pieces in Florida, and he now continued with some part-songs for mixed voices and with some orchestral works, the tone poem *Hiawatha, Sleigh Ride, Marche Caprice,* and a *Florida Suite,* which contains the well-known *La Calinda,* later incorporated into the opera *Koanga. La Calinda* is a charming piece in the style of a negro folk dance, and it has survived into the present-day repertory. But these early works are not really characteristic of the mature Delius; his personality had yet to emerge.

Delius continued to be drawn to Scandinavian culture and sought advice from Edward Grieg, who was in Leipzig at that time. Grieg strongly recommended that he devote himself entirely to music; this was the start of a long and firm friendship. Delius returned to Bradford in 1888, and Grieg came to London for a concert of his works; Delius was able to introduce his father to him. As a result of this meeting, and of Grieg's praise for his son, Delius senior agreed that his son should be allowed to stay in Europe for a period of time to develop as a composer.

Delius now moved to Paris, where he had an ally in Uncle Theodore, who supplemented the meagre allowance Delius received from his father. While there Delius wrote a variety of works: a number of songs, a melodrama and a setting of Ibsen's *Paa Vidderne* for speaker and orchestra. These he sent to Grieg, who made some helpful comments, pointing out the dangers always present in any combination of speaking voice with orchestra. In 1889 he wrote another orchestral suite and some more songs, mainly on Scandinavian texts.

In July he visited Norway with Grieg and Christian Sinding, a friend and fellow pupil, going up into remote mountain areas. There he decided that the subject of his first opera must be connected with the world of folklore and fairyland. This was to be *Irmelin,* a combination of two old legends, *The Princess and the Swineherd* and *Irmelin.*

Irmelin is an early mediæval heroine who resembles Turandot in her rejection of suitors, but is by no means so bloodthirsty in her behaviour. Delius wrote both the libretto and the music for this work, which kept him occupied until some time in 1892.

The years in Paris were rich in experiences and friendships. Delius took part in both the high life and the low life of the city. He did not, however, associate much with people in musical circles, although he knew the composers Florent Schmitt, who made the piano scores of his first two operas, and Ravel, who did the same for his third opera. He also met Strindberg and Gauguin, from whom he bought the painting *Nevermore* at a cost of about twenty pounds.

In January 1896 he met Jelka Rosen, who was to become his wife. She was from an old Schleswig-Holstein family, and had come to Paris to study painting. Though Jelka seems to have decided immediately that Delius was the only man in the world for her, Delius had many other women friends. He grew accustomed to working mostly at night, as he could not bear the noise of the day, and would stay up late drinking and smoking while he worked.

During the summer Delius sketched out the first two acts of *Koanga,* which depicted Negro life on a plantation; in August he once again visited Norway. Back in Paris in the autumn, he continued with *Koanga* and also made the first sketches for his piano concerto and the symphonic poem *Paris.* On visiting Delius at Christmas, Jelka was alarmed to hear that he was proposing to go to Florida for several months. Jelka would have been more alarmed had she known that one of Delius's lady friends from Parisian society was to appear on the same ship, travelling to New York disguised as a young man, and accompany him to Florida. At the end of June, Delius returned to Paris. He came down to Grez, a village about ten miles from Paris where Jelka lived, and took lodgings there. During the summer he worked on the third act of *Koanga* and his tone-poem *Over the Hills and Far Away.*

Delius's association with Norway was to continue, bringing him both notoriety and success. Having been invited to write incidental music for the Norwegian political comedy *Folkeraadet* (*Parliament*), he was conducting it in Oslo when a university student fired a blank cartridge at him. Delius at once fled from the pit and the theatre, seeking refuge in the Grand Hotel, where the venerable Ibsen comforted him; ultimately the play was a great success and was sold out for the next three weeks.

Returning from Norway, Delius stopped at Elberfeld in Germany to hear the first performance of *Over the Hills and Far Away*. The reception of the work was decidedly hostile; it was regarded as revolutionary, and the town council threatened to dismiss Dr Haym, the conductor, if he repeated the offence. Why it should have provoked this reaction seems obscure, for the work is orthodox in form and its harmonies should not have proved unusual to listeners accustomed to Wagner and the earlier works of Strauss; it is in fact an unusual (for Delius) coupling of serene passages with livelier and more extrovert music.

Once again the composer returned to Grez, which he now began to regard as a permanent home. A creative period followed: he finished the last act of *Koanga*, and the original version of the *Piano Concerto*. In 1898 there followed *The Dance Goes On* (the original version of *Life's Dance*), the *Night Song of Zarathustra* (later part of the *Mass of Life*), and replanned *Paris* and *Appalachia*, the latter being an earlier set of variations on a tune which Delius had heard the Negroes singing in the Florida tobacco factories.

Delius was always at his happiest in variation form, for it enabled him to express his ideas in a concise shape, and in *Appalachia* the music grows from the beginning through each successive variation, with the chorus playing an increasingly important part as the work goes on, to the final choral statement of the theme and the climax of the work, after which the music dies away in Delius's typical manner. *Koanga* is unlike Delius's other operas, being more 'operatic' in the conventional sense despite its Spanish-Negro setting; the characters fail to emerge as real people and therefore the work has failed to remain in the repertoire. The best music is to be found in the third act, which was written later than the other two; the mystical element of voodoo in the plot hardly has the terrifying effect which was intended.

With something of a reputation established abroad, Delius planned to give a concert of his works in London in the late spring of 1899. Despite the fact that the press was friendly, considering that not a note by Delius had ever been performed in England, the concert brought him little recognition in his native country, and none of his compositions was heard there for the next eight years.

In 1902, faced with the necessity of earning some money, Delius wrote a one-act opera, *Margot la Rouge,* for a competition sponsored by Ricordi. It was a shocker in the *verismo* style and not a work Delius really believed in; not unexpectedly it failed to win the prize. In the summer of 1903 Delius married Jelka Rosen.

Although his finances were far from secure, Delius thrived musically. In 1903 he wrote one of his finest works, *Sea Drift,* and in the following year began the *Mass of Life.* Success continued to come from abroad – this time from Germany, where *Koanga* and the *Piano Concerto* were performed in Elberfeld in 1904. *Appalachia* followed there the same year and made a startling impression.

Two great English conductors were to become associated with Delius's growing success in his homeland: Henry Wood had helped him in his first efforts to gain recognition, and now he was to meet the conductor who has always been associated with his work, Thomas Beecham.

Beecham has described his first impressions of Delius: 'He must be a cardinal or at least a bishop in mufti, I kept on saying to myself, for his features had that noble cast of asceticism and shrewdness one mentally associates with high-ranking ecclesiastics'. Beecham also described his style of speech: 'Not for him was the blameless diction so laboriously inculcated and standardized in our leading public schools and ancient universities. He loyally preserved his preference for the Doric dialect of the great northern county of broad acres.... Upon this had been grafted a polyglot mish-mash'.

By now Delius's works were receiving many performances, both in England and in Germany. Beecham gave the first English performance of *A Village Romeo and Juliet* at Covent Garden in 1910, but while it attracted some attention, most of the public was dazzled by the performance in the same season of Strauss's *Elektra.* Based on Gottfried Keller's story of two young lovers whose families quarrel over the ownership of a piece of land and who wish to go together away from the world, *A Village Romeo and Juliet* has a curiously dreamlike quality which is not dramatic in the orthodox sense but is full of atmosphere. The music has been accused of being too static, and it is true that a lot of it moves slowly, apart from certain passages such as the fair scene; but it has an individual beauty of a 'sunset' kind which earned it success in British and European opera houses, and the interlude *The Walk to the Paradise Garden* still remains in the concert repertory.

Meanwhile Delius continued to compose; in 1912 he wrote what is perhaps his most famous piece, *On Hearing the First Cuckoo in Spring* for small orchestra: a short nature poem of great beauty, concisely written and partly based on a Norwegian folk tune which he had been given by Grieg. But combined with the welcoming spring is a feeling of sadness; spring has so little time to stay. This mood is characteristic of much of Delius's music.

In 1913–14 he produced *Four North Country Sketches* for orchestra. Life was not to remain peaceful; the war of 1914 came as a great shock to Delius and his wife. Forced by the rapid advances of the Germans to leave Grez, they eventually arrived in England, where Beecham was able to provide them with a small house near Watford. Here Delius began a work about which much argument has raged, the

Requiem; he was not a Christian, and he wrote the text for this work himself. It was first performed in 1922 under Albert Coates, and was a failure, but it was revived in 1966 with considerable success. Delius has been criticised for attacking Christian philosophy in this work – during the First World War this was considered not quite the thing to do – in favour of a pagan point of view. The *Requiem* contains a good deal of fine music – even its critics praise the opening funeral march and the soprano elegy in the second part – and it is more definite and concise than much of Delius's music. In an age which is more attuned than that of fifty years ago to the sentiments of his text it can hope for more successful performances.

In 1919 the theatrical producer, Basil Dean, commissioned music for James Elroy Flecker's *Hassan.* Delius wrote a score which contains some of his most original music; apart from the well-known *Serenade* and the final choral section, *The Golden Journey to Samarkand*, there are effective and forceful choruses for beggars and soldiers, and a striking orchestral movement, *The Procession of Protracted Death.*

Delius was always at his best when he had a definite idea to portray, and for this reason was very much at home in the theatre when the texts he was asked to illustrate suited him. The colourful, but also cruel, oriental atmosphere of *Hassan* clearly stimulated him; however he did not write bogus 'Arab' music, but instead broadened his normal style and made it more varied and dramatic. The ballet music is far more exciting rhythmically than anything he had written for years, and the music for the ghost scene has a strange and curious atmosphere; one could wish that Delius had written more for the theatre.

In 1921 the French Government had made good the damage caused by the troops at his house at Grez, and he and Jelka returned there and remained until the end of the year.

It was then that Delius began to suffer from the illness

which was to last the rest of his life – the results of the venereal disease which he had contracted in his earlier Paris years. He went in January 1922 to a sanatorium in Wiesbaden, and from there carried on a long correspondence with the Hungarian composers Bartók and Kodály. Bartók in particular was a great admirer of Delius's work and often sent him compositions of his own. Bartók was much impressed by the *Mass of Life,* which he heard in Vienna, and both he and Kodály were very interested in the unaccompanied choruses that Delius had written during the war. These had no words, and Bartók regarded them as a new medium of a very original kind.

In 1923 Delius's health improved somewhat. He attended the première of *Hassan* in London, in September, a lavishly staged production with choreography by Fokine. The play was most successful, and ran for months in London and in the provinces.

By 1925 Delius was totally blind. He was also no longer able to walk and had to be carried up and down the stairs in the house in Grez, to which he and Jelka had now returned. Here he remained immobilized for the rest of his life, apart from a visit to London for the Delius Festival of 1929. He was able to hear and speak, and musicians played to him; he listened to the radio and to gramophone records, and Jelka and others read innumerable books aloud to him. It is interesting that his taste in music was very limited; apart from his own works, he would listen only to Chopin, Wagner and Grieg. When a well-known string quartet offered to play a Beethoven quartet, he shouted at them: 'Oh no you don't!'

In the spring of 1933 he received a visit from Elgar, whom he had never previously known well. This led to a warm friendship between the two men, and a correspondence which continued until the deaths of both of them in the following year. Elgar wrote to Delius about his admiration for *A Mass of Life,* and said: 'It has been a matter of no small amusement to me that as my name, somewhat unfortunately, is indissolubly connected with 'sacred' music, some of your friends and mine tried to make me believe that I am ill disposed to the trend and sympathy of your great work. Nothing could be further from the real truth of the case. I admire your work intensely and salute the genius displayed in it!'.

Elgar and Delius were the last poets of the romantic age in England, as well as being the first English composers of this century to win international reputations. Elgar had his patriotic and military side, reflecting the glories of an empire which was soon to fade away, but his real character was expressed in his many passages of lyrical nostalgia. Delius was the poet of nature, of the high hills and the sunset; nearly all his works end quietly as if, like himself, they mourn an age which was about to vanish forever. The foundation of a truly English style of music was not to come until the next generation, with the work of Vaughan Williams and Holst.

2 The English nationalist school

Nationalism in music was a product of the nineteenth century. Its origins were partly political; in Czechoslovakia and Hungary, for instance, native composers revolted against the Germanic culture imported by the occupying Austrians. They wished to create a national music of their own, based on their folk-songs and using their own language. The melodies and rhythms of native folk-songs influenced even the symphonic works of Smetana and Dvořák in Czechoslovakia, and even a cosmopolitan composer like Liszt was very much affected by the music of his native Hungary. In other countries, too, music began to grow more nationalistic in revolt against the cosmopolitan culture which usually flourished at the courts; thus in Russia the nationalist school under Balakirev wrote Russian music based on Russian and even Caucasian folk-songs in order to replace the French and Italian influences in music favoured by the Imperial Court. Similarly, in Norway a nationalist school grew up with Grieg at its head which spoke in a different voice from the German music which was then prevalent. In England where, as we have seen, German influences were dominant throughout the nineteenth century, the nationalist tide did not begin to flow until the beginning of the twentieth century, and the leading figures in this movement were two very dissimilar composers, Ralph Vaughan Williams and Gustav Holst, who nevertheless shared common aims.

Both Vaughan Williams and Holst were certain that it was English folk-song which had liberated music in England from the German tradition and given it a voice of its own. Vaughan Williams once wrote: 'My intercourse with Cecil Sharp (the pioneer collector of British folk-songs) crystallised and confirmed what I already vaguely felt about folk-song and its relationship to the composer's art. With him you had to be either pro-folk-song or anti-folk-song, and I came down heavily on the folk-song side'. This was the basis of his famous article, published in 1912; 'Who wants the British composer?'[1] And Imogen Holst declared of her father: 'The other important event (of 1905) was the revival of folk-song. Folk-songs finally brushed all trace of Wagner from his work. He had the deepest admiration for Cecil Sharp and felt that when the time came for the English musical history of the twentieth century to be written, Cecil Sharp's name would stand out above all others'. Frank Howes, in his book *The English Musical Renaissance,* points out that 'other influences besides folk-song operated in the formation of both men's respective styles. In the case of Vaughan Williams, one was the hymn tunes he examined for his edition of the English hymnal. In that of Holst it was Weelkes and Purcell, which he made his various choirs sing. Both were touched by the new interest in plain-song, and both found in Bach an antidote to too much Beethoven and Wagner'. Both were interested in writing for amateurs, including choral societies and brass bands, and in musical education – they possessed a social as well as an artistic conscience.

Ralph Vaughan Williams came of mixed Welsh and English blood. His father was born into a legal family from Wales; his grandfather was a judge who settled with his family at Leith Hill, near Dorking. The house next door belonged to the Wedgwood family, descendants of the famous potter, who had also intermarried with the Darwins

(Charles Darwin was Vaughan Williams's great uncle). The two households soon developed a close friendship, and in 1868 Arthur Vaughan Williams married Margaret Wedgwood. Arthur was a clergyman, and had the living of Down Ampney in Gloucestershire. He had three children; Ralph, the third, was born at Down Ampney on 12 October 1872. Arthur died only two and a half years later and Margaret brought her family back to her parents' house in Leith Hill. Here Vaughan Williams was brought up and was given music lessons by his aunt. He learnt first the piano and then the violin. He went to Charterhouse in 1887 where he played the viola in the school orchestra and sang in the school choir. In the summer of 1890 he was able to go to Munich to hear Wagner's operas for the first time. In the same year he entered the Royal College of Music, where he remained for two years, and in 1892 went up to Trinity College, Cambridge.

At Cambridge his official subject was history, but he continued his lessons at the Royal College of Music. During this period he met a number of men with whom he formed lifelong friendships: the philosopher G. E. Moore, the historian G. M. Trevelyan and H. P. Allen, later Sir Hugh Allen, director of the Royal College of Music.

Although an allowance from his family made it unnecessary for him to earn his living, he took an organist's post at Lambeth in London. He had become engaged to Adeline Fisher; they were married in October 1897 and went to Berlin. Here Vaughan Williams studied with Max Bruch, returning in April of the following year to London and his organist's position in Lambeth, which left him time to write music of his own, including a setting of Matthew Arnold's *Dover Beach.* Some of his song settings, among them *Linden Lea,* which was to become well-known, stem from this period. Though he had not yet achieved a really mature style in these, it was clear that he was reacting against German influences, which he found actually repugnant; apart from folk song, the chief influence on his music was

1 Edward Elgar (1857–1934), the first distinguished composer to emerge in England after the Victorian era. This picture dates from about 1905, when he announced that he had no more desire to write music; twenty productive years followed.

2 Elgar and Mrs John Drinkwater at George Bernard Shaw's garden party (Malvern, August 1932).

3 Frederick Delius (1862–1934) in middle age: the conductor Thomas Beecham, who worked tirelessly on his behalf, said he resembled 'a cardinal or at least a bishop in mufti'.

4 Delius, in his last years, with his wife Jelka.

5 Ralph Vaughan Williams (1872–1958), England's leading nationalist composer, as a young man.

6 Vaughan Williams (centre) at the diamond jubilee of the English Folk Dance and Song Society (16 May 1958) with the director, Douglas Kennedy (left) and the Australian composer Percy Grainger (right).

7 Gustav Holst (1874–1934) and his wife Isobel. Holst was Vaughan Williams's friend and collaborator, and his suite *The Planets* is a popular classic.

8 Arthur Bliss (b. 1891), Master of the Queen's Musick (left), with the French composer Honegger (centre) at the 1959 Bergen Festival.

9 William Walton (b. 1902), regarded between the wars as the *enfant terrible* of English music, conducting the London Symphony Orchestra.

that of the Elizabethan composers, Purcell and even mediaeval music at times. He also admired Parry for his mastery of choral technique. It was at this period that he began to think about composing a large choral work with the sea as its subject. This was eventually to become the *Sea Symphony.*

It was a period when great interest was shown in collecting folk music, and Bartók and Kodály were beginning their collections of Hungarian folk-songs. 1903 saw the beginning of Vaughan Williams's collection of English folk-songs, in which he collaborated with Cecil Sharp.

In 1905 he began the first of his mature works, a setting of Walt Whitman's poem *Toward the Unknown Region.* He still felt that he was not sufficiently equipped as a composer, and he travelled to Paris to study with Ravel. Ravel helped him to refine his style, concentrating on lessons in orchestration. Vaughan Williams wrote of this experience: 'As far as I know my own faults he hit them all exactly and is telling me to do exactly what I half felt in my mind I ought to do'. Ravel took a keen interest in the English composer, and the two remained friends for many years.

The time spent with Ravel must have given Vaughan Williams the confidence he needed to complete larger, orchestral works. The *Sea Symphony* was first performed at the Leeds Festival in October 1910, and made a tremendous impression. It is a setting for soloists, chorus and orchestra of several poems about the sea by Walt Whitman, in four movements resembling those of the classical symphony, though the form of each movement is often dictated by the structure of the words. It is a powerful work which also contains many beautiful lyrical moments, though the finale is perhaps too extended to balance the rest. It was then that Vaughan Williams met Isadora Duncan and began work on a choral ballet based on *The Bacchae* for her. And always much concerned with the richness of English folk culture, he gave a lecture early in 1912 in which he set forward his ideas on English folk music: 'The evolution of the English

folk-song by itself has ceased but its spirit can continue to grow and flourish at the hand of our native composers ... we have made the mistake in England of trying to take over "ready-made" a foreign culture, a culture which is the result of generations of patient development, and of attempting to fit on to it our own incompatible conditions. This is merely to reap where we have not sown and the result must be failure'.

His *London Symphony* was first performed on 27 March 1914 in a concert of modern orchestral music conducted by Geoffrey Toye at the Queen's Hall. 'A better title', wrote Vaughan Williams, 'would perhaps be Symphony by a Londoner, that is to say, the life of London (including possibly its various sights and sounds) has suggested to the composer an attempt at musical expression, but it would be no help to the hearer to describe these in words.' And in fact the music does contain various London sounds such as the Westminster chimes, a theme derived from the street-cry 'sweet lavender', the sound of a mouth-organ and the jingle of hansom bells; but these are all worked into a true symphonic structure in four movements, and only appear incidentally. Although the piece enjoyed great success, the composer was unable to find an English publisher, so he sent his only score to Breitkopf and Härtel in Leipzig.

As soon as war broke out, Vaughan Williams enlisted in the Royal Army Medical Corps, although he was over forty. In June 1916 his unit left for France, where they were stationed at Écoives. It was here that the ideas for *A Pastoral Symphony* had their origin; the long trumpet cadenza in the second movement owed its inspiration to a bugler who used to practise in the evening. In the autumn the unit embarked for Salonika; Vaughan Williams remained with it till early 1917, when someone in authority arranged for him to be sent back to England to train for a commission. He said: 'My only regret at leaving is that I shall cease to be a man and become an officer'.

Peace brought with it a new period of success. On returning to London, he was invited to teach at the Royal College of Music. He was made an honorary Doctor of Music at Oxford, and his *Sea Symphony* was performed on that occasion in celebration of the two hundred and fiftieth anniversary of the opening of the Sheldonian Theatre. The unaccompanied *Mass in G Minor* belongs to that period. Of the latter he said: 'There is no reason why an atheist could not write a good mass'.

During the next six years he completed many works and was working on his opera based on Falstaff, *Sir John in Love*. In 1929 he wrote a *Fantasia* for cello and orchestra for Pablo Casals, as well as a concerto for two violins. By now Vaughan Williams's mature style had been fully developed. One could describe it as a mixture of modal harmonies and melodies derived from folk song with polytonal counterpoint and a fondness for moving in block chords. This style was characteristic of him for the rest of his life, though certain of his later works show a rather more austere character.

As early as 1927 he had begun work on the ballet *Job*. The scenario had been provided by Geoffrey Keynes, and the work had originally been intended for Diaghilev who, however, thought the idea 'too English', as it was based on Blake's illustrations to the Book of Job. With no immediate prospects of a stage production Vaughan Williams designed the work as an orchestral suite, in somewhat expanded form, for the Norwich Festival. Meanwhile, however, the Camargo Society had become interested in it after Ninette de Valois and Lilian Baylis had seen the model sets and designs, and the ballet was first performed by the Camargo Society in July 1931 at the Cambridge Theatre.

In the winter of 1931–2 Vaughan Williams began a new symphony, his fourth. It was first performed on 10 April 1935 by Adrian Boult and the BBC Orchestra; it was a more powerful and violent work than anything he had written before, and remains one of his most original pieces. It is very much more chromatic and dissonant than his usual pastoral style and has a mood of bitterness which is absent from most of his other works. Vaughan Williams may have been thinking subconsciously of the conflict between good and evil in *Job,* but he seems to have been stirred to write the work after reading an account of a 'modernistic' symphony given at one of the International Society for Contemporary Music's festivals. It ends with a fugal epilogue which sums up the whole work, based on a motto theme of four notes which are also heard in inversion and are combined with other subjects of the finale; and there is a final reference to the opening bars of the first movement.

Shortly after the first performance he was offered the Order of Merit; although he had previously refused all honours, he was prepared to accept this. During the summer he was engaged on three major works, the *Five Tudor Portraits* for chorus and orchestra to texts by John Skelton, the fifteenth-century poet, a comic opera *The Poisoned Kiss,* and another choral work, *Dona Nobis Pacem.* The text of this last work was a setting of three poems by Walt Whitman, and this certainly was a clear presentiment of the coming world war.

Vaughan Williams had now started another symphony, using music which he had been accumulating for a full-scale opera, *Pilgrim's Progress,* which he felt he would never finish. During this pre-war period he was awarded the Shakespeare Prize by an anonymous Hamburg merchant; he accepted this with some misgivings, and in his letter of acceptance wrote that he would agree to have it only if it implied no support of German politics and if he would be free to hold and express any views he wished on the general state of Germany. However, by 1939 his music was on Hitler's black list, probably because his name appeared on many liberal and anti-Nazi committees.

About this time he received some suggestions for ballet scenarios, one based on Spenser's *Epithalamion* from Ursula Wood. After a long correspondence they met for the first time in early 1938. They soon became friends, and she was in fact later to become his second wife.

The wartime period was to see a development of Vaughan Williams's political commitment to individual liberty. Late in 1938 he joined the Dorking Committee for Refugees from Nazi Oppression and took a full share in its work. His idealism moved him to take a stand against injustices; when Alan Bush's music had been banned by the BBC because of his Communist activities, Vaughan Williams at once wrote to the BBC, saying that although he himself disagreed with Bush's political views, he wished to protest against this victimization of private opinion, and therefore requested the BBC to return to him the choral song he had composed for them. He himself returned his fee for it. Later, in 1943, he spoke in favour of Michael Tippett, then Director of Music at Morley College, before a tribunal which had sentenced him to prison for refusing to do agricultural work, even though he did not agree with Tippett's pacifist views.

In 1940 Vaughan Williams undertook composing for a new medium, films. At the suggestion of his former pupil, Muir Mathieson, Director of Music at London Films, he wrote the music for his first film, *The Forty-Ninth Parallel.* This was shown with great success in 1941, and as a result he was asked to write music for two further films, *Coastal Command* and *The People's Land.*

From this time dates a long and interesting letter to a friend who had sought advice on a possible musical career for his son. This letter, contained in Ursula Vaughan Williams's biography of her husband, gave the advice that a young composer should take part in as much practical music-making as possible, study the great masters, and work at home, going abroad only when mature. Vaughan Williams, always reacting against any form of pomposity, calmly answered Walford Davies, who said that he had written his *Solemn Melody* on his knees, 'I write my music on my bottom'.

The fifth symphony, more pastoral in style than its predecessor, had been completed and Vaughan Williams conducted its first performance at a Promenade Concert on 24 June 1943.

Advanced age did not diminish the composer's energies. In 1944 he provided incidental music for *Richard II* for the BBC, and wrote an oboe concerto for Leon Goossens. After the war ended, he began his sixth symphony. Early in 1948 its first performance was given at a Royal Philharmonic concert; like the fourth symphony, it is a powerful and dramatic work, and many people felt that it was not only inspired by the war, but also that the quiet and sinister last movement represented earth after total destruction by atomic bombs. Vaughan Williams, however, said that the last movement was based on Prospero's speech from *The Tempest*: 'The cloud-capp'd towers, the gorgeous palaces, the solemn temples, the great globe itself . . . shall dissolve and . . . leave not a wrack behind'.

In May 1951 Adeline died. After her death, Vaughan Williams asked Ursula Wood to help him with his domestic affairs. In the summer of 1952 they spent a holiday in France together. Early the next year they married.

Though Vaughan Williams was close to eighty, his creative energies did not flag; he wrote a *Romance* for harmonica and orchestra for Larry Adler, and a seventh symphony, the *Sinfonia Antartica,* partly based on his music for the film *Scott of the Antarctic.* In the summer of 1955, after a holiday in Greece, he gave a lecture in Cork, in which he attempted to prove that almost all the good Irish (not Gaelic) folk-songs were really derived from England; his audience was naturally somewhat outraged. The eighth symphony, on which Vaughan Williams had been working for some time, had its first performance at Manchester under Barbirolli in May 1956; the score is notable for its inclusion of a number of tuned gongs. He had already started on a ninth symphony, and continued to work on it while on a summer holiday in Majorca. In 1957, while on holiday in Austria, he heard a flugel horn for the first time and decided to incorporate it in his new ninth symphony. He lived through a major operation, and his eighty-fifth birthday, in October, was celebrated with a concert of his works at the Festival Hall.

After a short holiday in Dorset in 1958 Vaughan Williams returned to London, and here, on 26 August 1958, he died suddenly of a coronary thrombosis.

By basing his melodic and harmonic style on English folk-song, Vaughan Williams was able to free English music from German influences; certain traces of a French style appeared instead, however, especially in his more lyrical works such as the *Pastoral* and fifth symphonies. He influenced many English composers over a period of forty to fifty years, the most notable of these being Herbert Howells (born in 1892), E. J. Moeran (1895–1950), Gordon Jacob (born 1895) and Gerald Finzi (1901–56).

Vaughan Williams's principal collaborator in the English folk-song school was Gustav Holst, born at Cheltenham on 21 September 1874. His great-grandfather was a Swedish musician who taught the harp to the Imperial Family at St Petersburg and left Russia with his wife and his small son early in the nineteenth century because of his political views. Later the son settled in Cheltenham. Both Holst's grandfather and father were musicians. His mother was English, and died when Holst was only eight. He was looked after by his father's sister, Nina, who was a keen musician.

Holst started early to play both violin and piano, and at the age of thirteen he had set the poem *Horatius* for chorus and orchestra. Later, when he was seventeen, he was given some counterpoint training at Oxford. Having tried unsuccessfully to win scholarships at various London colleges of music, he returned to Cheltenham, where he obtained an organist's job at a village in the Cotswolds. He was given the conductorship of a local choral society, and wrote an operetta, *Lansdowne Castle,* which was produced in 1893 in Cheltenham with great success. As a result, his father borrowed a hundred pounds from one of his relations and sent Holst to the Royal College of Music.

At the College he studied composition with Stanford, and soon became a great admirer of Wagner. About this time neuritis in his right hand made him give up the piano; instead he took up the trombone, which enabled him to earn his living as an orchestral player. Hoping to cure his neuritis he became a vegetarian and a teetotaller, but in fact this only seemed to increase the weakness of his eyes, from which he had suffered since his childhood. In 1894 he won an open scholarship in composition, which enabled him to stay on at the College. He supplemented his income by playing the trombone on the pier at Brighton and other seaside resorts. In the autumn of 1895, just after his twenty-first birthday, he met Vaughan Williams for the first time; they soon became friends and got into the habit of playing each other their works. Holst was writing an opera called *The Revoke*. He became interested in socialism and ran the Hammersmith Socialist Club, attending Bernard Shaw's lectures at Kelmscott House.

In 1897 he was asked to conduct the Socialist Choir, and there he met his future wife, Isobel Harrison, who sang in the choir as a soprano. He earned a living as organist in several churches in London, and continued to play the trombone in various theatre orchestras. In the autumn of 1898, however, the Carl Rosa Opera company offered him an appointment as first trombone and repetiteur. His work with the Carl Rosa company gave him a much more intimate knowledge of opera and invaluable insight into orchestration. He was becoming interested in Sanskrit literature and although he was never converted to any religion, Hinduism appealed to him very strongly. He thought of setting some Sanskrit hymns to music, but the words of the usual English versions were far too stilted. Not to be stopped, he managed to learn enough Sanskrit to translate twenty hymns from the *Rig Veda* and also wrote his own libretti for the operas *Sita* and *Savitri*. He began the music of *Sita* in 1900; during this year he was able to finish his *Suite in E Flat* for orchestra, a *Cotswold Symphony* and an *Ave Maria* in eight parts for unaccompanied women's chorus.

Holst married Isobel Harrison in the summer of 1902, and coming into a small legacy on the death of his father, he and his wife were at last able to afford a honeymoon: in the spring of 1903 they went to Berlin.

On returning to England, Holst decided to give up trombone playing and to devote his life to composition. His first efforts were a good many songs, invariably rejected by publishers. But he was soon able to begin his career as a teacher and in 1905 was appointed Director of Music at St Paul's Girls' School in Hammersmith, a post which he held until his death. He began to be interested in English folk-song and wrote his *Country Song* and *Marching Song* for orchestra, as well as sketching his *Somerset Rhapsody*. The influence of folk-song in these early works is fairly slight though they do contain some modal elements.

He continued his Sanskrit studies, and by 1907 had finished the music of *Sita* and was beginning to set the first group of hymns from the *Rig Veda.* That year Holst was appointed musical director at Morley College for Working Men and Women. Here he revolutionized the musical curriculum and began to build it up to the high standard which it still has today.

In 1908 he was bitterly disappointed when *Sita* failed to win the Ricordi Opera Prize; severe neuritis and overwork had reduced him to such a state of nerves that his doctor ordered him to take a holiday in a warm climate. He borrowed some money from a friend and went to Algeria, where he bicycled in the desert. As soon as he returned home, he began writing *Savitri,* his second Indian opera. *Sita* has never been published; *Savitri,* a one-act chamber opera for three singers, wordless chorus and a small instrumental ensemble, is written in an austere style with some elements derived from oriental music, such as augmented intervals and modal scales. It is very effective dramatically: not a note is wasted, and Holst manages to achieve a great variety of colour with limited resources.

In the summer of 1913 the new music wing at St Paul's was opened, and Holst was given a large sound-proof room to work in. Working mostly on Sundays, he wrote the *St Paul's Suite* for the school orchestra as a token of his gratitude. His earlier interest in Hinduism gradually gave way to one in astrology, and this became the point of departure for his new work, *The Planets.* He had just finished the sketch of *Mars, the bringer of war,* when war in fact broke out, in 1914; Holst at once tried to enlist, but was turned down because of his neuritis and weak sight.

The Planets is a large-scale suite for full orchestra which contains a great variety of styles, ranging from the savagery of *Mars,* the delicacy of *Venus,* the scherzo-like character of *Mercury* and the mysticism of *Uranus* to the remoteness of *Neptune.* This variety however does not mean that the composer's personality is lost: there is always an astringency and power in his handling of his material. *The Planets* has remained Holst's best-known work.

In the summer of 1917 he set the *Hymn of Jesus,* from the *Apocrypha,* and for this purpose he taught himself Greek so as to be able to understand the original. Long wanting to take a more active part in war work, he was at last offered the job of musical organizer to the YMCA among the troops in the Near East.

Returning from the Near East and back at St Paul's, he began setting Walt Whitman's *Ode to Death* for chorus and orchestra, struggling at the same time to write the libretto of his opera *The Perfect Fool.* Meanwhile *The Hymn of Jesus* had been published in the Carnegie Collection of British Music, and Holst conducted its first public performance at the Queen's Hall in March 1920. This had an overwhelming reception – Holst was becoming successful at last. But Holst was never very good at public relations and simply did not know how to deal with press photographers or journalists, as well as consistently refusing to accept any honours, degrees or titles.

Early in 1923, while rehearsing at Reading, he slipped off the platform and fell, landing on the back of his head. Though he recovered quickly at the time, this injury was to cause him trouble in later years. In the early summer, he travelled to the University of Michigan at Ann Arbor to conduct a music festival. Meanwhile *The Perfect Fool* had been performed at Covent Garden under Eugene Goossens. This opera somewhat puzzled the critics, who did not realize that it was intended as a parody of various operatic styles, notably Verdi and Wagner: it contains two characters, the Troubadour and the Traveller, who contend for the hand of the Princess to suitable music: she however prefers the Fool, who sleeps through nearly all the action of the opera – an obvious dig at *Parsifal.*

While in the USA Holst was offered a professorship at Ann Arbor but felt he could not accept it as he did not have the energy to undertake the duties involved. He returned to England in June to hear *The Perfect Fool* and *Savitri* at Covent Garden, and in the autumn conducted *The Planets* and his new *Fugal Concerto* twice at the Queen's Hall to packed houses.

Success notwithstanding, his nerves were now in a bad state through overwork. When an anonymous rich patron offered him several hundred pounds to give him leisure for composing, he gave up nearly all his teaching for the next few months and began working on a new symphony. Although he found it difficult to teach composition theoretically, he was attached to his teaching at Morley and St Paul's; he was able to build up the performances of the students and inspire them with genuine enthusiasm for the music he liked. Now living alone at Thaxted, looked after by a manservant, he wrote his *Choral Symphony,* settings of poems by Keats. Admittedly it is difficult to make a setting of the *Ode on a Grecian Urn* which can add much to the poetry of the words, and the last movement, *Bards of passion and of mirths* is rather on the long side, but the first movement's Bacchanal in 7/8 time and the Scherzo, *Fancy* and *Folly's Song* are both delightful and exciting, and it seems a pity that this work is performed so rarely nowadays.

About the same time he began a new short opera *At the Boar's Head,* an interlude based on the Falstaff scenes from *Henry V*; it was built to a great extent on Morris and country dance tunes which happened to fit Shakespeare's words.

The *Choral Symphony* was performed at the Leeds Festival in October 1925 and, three weeks later, at the Queen's Hall. It was not a great success, and Holst was bitterly disappointed, especially as Vaughan Williams wrote to say that he felt a 'cold admiration' for it.

Holst was a close friend of Robert Bridges and Thomas Hardy, and was now inspired by the latter's *Return of the Native* to write an orchestral piece, *Egdon Heath,* one of his most interesting and remarkable works. The music catches the austere and remote quality of Hardy's description of the scene, and a good deal of it is more experimental harmonically than anything Holst had written before – so much so that listeners to its first performance failed to understand it, and its true stature has only been appreciated in recent years.

During the summer he was unwell and at the end of the year he decided to stop work and have three months' holiday in Italy. On returning to England he was as active as ever. In 1930 he finished a *Concerto for Two Violins* for the sisters Jelly d'Aranyi and Adila Fachiri. The concerto was played at a Philharmonic concert at the Queen's Hall in April, and on the same occasion Holst was presented with the Gold Medal of the Royal Philharmonic Society. He was working on his *Choral Fantasia,* in homage to Robert Bridges, as well as on *Hammersmith,* a Prelude and Scherzo originally commissioned by the BBC Military Band, and afterwards rewritten for orchestra. His sixth and last opera, *The Tale of the Wandering Scholar,* with a libretto by

Clifford Bax, was written in 1930. After all this activity, 1931 found him exhausted. In the summer he went to the Three Choirs Festival at Gloucester for the first performance of his *Choral Fantasia*. This received poor notices from the press, but Holst was cheered by an offer from Harvard University to act as lecturer in composition for the first six months of 1932, and also by one from Boston to conduct their Symphony Orchestra in three concerts of his own works. He left England at the beginning of January, and the concerts at Boston were a great success. At Harvard he was able to start composing again, but at the end of March suffered a severe attack of haemorrhagic gastritis; he spent a fortnight in hospital. He was taken ill again at Christmas and spent the next few months in and out of a nursing home. After six weeks in the nursing home he was told that the treatment had not cured him; he could have a minor operation, which would probably be successful but would mean his leading a restricted life, or a major operation, which would be serious and possibly dangerous. He chose the latter. For the next few months he relaxed. In May 1934 he was operated on; the operation was successful but his heart could not stand the strain, and he died on 25 May.

Holst was a composer of a remarkably original turn of mind, and he absorbed many influences. English folk-song was by no means the only one, and to some extent he was an eclectic. He made a notable contribution to English music although this is only just beginning to be appreciated today. In many ways he was in advance of his time, and the austerity of many of his works is more in keeping with modern music than with the somewhat lusher and more romantic style of his contemporaries.

Three other English composers of this generation deserve to be mentioned; although they were not so directly affected by English folk-song as Vaughan Williams and Holst, they definitely represent a nationalist school in that they wished to eradicate German influences from English music, however much they admired the German classics themselves.

The eldest of these was Frank Bridge (1879–1941), whose contribution was mainly in the field of chamber music, although he also wrote a small number of orchestral works. Beginning as a romantic, his style became increasingly 'modern' during the 1930s, especially in such works as his *Divertimenti* for wind quartet and his later chamber music, which show an experimental use of harmony. He is also remembered for his teaching of Benjamin Britten.

John Ireland (1879–1962) is also chiefly remembered for his chamber music and songs, though he wrote an important piano concerto which still remains in the repertoire. His other works show a genuinely individual gift, and his settings of the poems of Hardy and Housman are extremely subtle. He had an extraordinary ability to reproduce the atmosphere of a poem in music by apparently simple means: he did not aim at bold effects, but his settings show a far more real understanding of his chosen poets than the more superficial ones of his contemporaries like Arthur Somervell, for instance. His music shows some influence of his French contemporaries, particularly Debussy, but he worked out an individual style which combines both English and French elements.

Arnold Bax (1883–1953) was very much a romantic: apart from his music he also attached himself to the 'Celtic twilight' school of literature, whose protagonists were Synge and Yeats, and he wrote prose under the name of Dermot O'Byrne. He is chiefly remembered for his seven symphonies, highly romantic and passionate and based partly on folk elements, but characterized by a certain turgid texture which has prevented them from becoming popular. He was a brilliant musician who could read any score at sight, and this possibly tempted him into over-writing. As a person, he was extremely quick-witted and astringent, in complete contrast to the romanticism of his music.

An interesting survivor from this period is Havergal Brian; he was born in 1877 and is still alive at the time of writing. Between the ages of seventy-eight and ninety-three he wrote no less than twenty-two symphonies, in addition to the ten which he composed earlier. Though stemming from the romantic style, his music is very much more austere and 'modern' than that of his contemporaries; many of his symphonies are one-movement works of fairly short duration, and he has added an entirely original element to English music. His principal virtue in his later works is compression and reduction of the music to its bare essentials; in achieving this he got away both from his romantic background and the folk-song school of his youth. His music is often harsh and violent in a manner which is well attuned to the present day.

3 British composers in the 1920s

After the First World War the younger British composers reacted against the previous generation; they were not interested in basing a national style on English folk-song and they had a very much more international outlook. One of the leaders in this movement, more by force of his personality than as a composer, was the Dutch-born composer Bernard Van Dieren, a pupil and friend of Busoni.

Van Dieren came to London in 1909 as musical correspondent for various continental papers, and remained there until the end of his life. He was born in 1884 and died at the early age of fifty-two in 1936. He was a man of remarkable personality who greatly impressed everyone he met. He wrote some atonal piano pieces in about 1910, but his later works show a more romantic type of harmony, though the music itself is highly contrapuntal, and often contains a number of complex strands. He wrote a large number of songs in various languages which show great sensitivity in the setting of the texts, and also a large-scale work for chorus and orchestra, his *Chinese Symphony*.

Another composer who influenced the young men of the twenties, again more as a personality than as a composer, was Peter Warlock, 1894–1930. Warlock's real name was Philip Heseltine; he invented the name Peter Warlock as a kind of second personality. As Cecil Gray has described him in his biography, Heseltine was a shy and sensitive character, while Warlock (the name means 'one in league with the devil') was a rumbustious, roistering, neo-Elizabethan personality. In general, Heseltine used his own name for his literary output, and signed his compositions 'Warlock'; but some of Warlock's compositions are clearly by Heseltine, one example being the song cycle *The Curlew*, sensitive settings of poems by Yeats. Though Warlock was internationally minded and was aware of the music being written on the Continent at that time, including the works of Alban Berg, the main influences on his music were the Elizabethan madrigalists and the chromatic harmony of Delius, whom he greatly admired. He was fascinated by the sixteenth and seventeenth centuries, and most of his songs use texts of that period, though he did a number of settings of modern poets as well. He edited a good deal of Elizabethan lute music and Purcell's string fantasies. In the end the war between the two sides of his nature became an insoluble problem and in 1930 he committed suicide, but not forgetting to put the cat out first.

The post-war British composers rebelled against the previous generation in several different ways. Apart from not being interested in English folk-song as such, they were also not academics in the sense of teaching in academies and colleges. Moreover, they were interested in continental influences and absorbed many of them, particularly that of Stravinsky. This was not the Stravinsky of *The Rite of Spring* but rather the small-scale Stravinsky of works like *The Soldier's Tale.* His influence made itself felt particularly in rhythmical freedom.

This generation of composers was more interested in the other arts than its predecessors. The oldest of the group, Arthur Bliss, who was born in 1891, had served with the Guards in the First World War; his immediate post-war works, such as *Conversations, Rout* and *Madame Noy,* show the influence of Stravinsky and are written for chamber groups. Later, however, he adopted a broader and more imposing manner, which can already be seen in the *Colour Symphony* of 1922, revised in 1932. This tendency was carried on in the choral symphony *Morning Heroes,* written in memory of 'my brother and all other comrades killed in battle'. The same may be said of his *Piano Concerto* of 1939, a brilliant work in the tradition of Liszt and Rachmaninov. In all these works, as well as in the very effective ballet *Checkmate,* he shows himself to be in the tradition of Elgar rather than of Stravinsky. But there is also a lyrical side to his nature, which can be seen in the *Oboe Quintet* of 1927, the *Clarinet Quintet* of 1931 and the *Pastoral* for chorus and orchestra. In 1953, Bliss was appointed Master of the Queen's Music, and he has written a certain amount of occasional music since then. In 1961 he wrote a large oratorio, *The Beatitudes.*

But the composers who appeared to be the real revolutionaries in those days were two younger men, William Walton and Constant Lambert. William Walton was born on 29 March 1902 at Oldham, Lancashire; his father taught singing. When Walton was ten his father happened to see an advertisement for a voice trial of probationary choristers at Christ Church, Oxford. His mother just managed to get him there in time after missing train connections from the North – an example of the luck which, according to Walton himself, has pursued him all his life. Walton was accepted and remained at the choir school from 1912 to 1918. He began to compose, chiefly motets for double chorus. Though he had no formal musical education, the fact of being a chorister at Christ Church was in itself an education, as he has said himself.

When Walton's voice broke, he was kept on by the Dean of Christ Church, Dr Thomas Strong, who allowed Walton to become an undergraduate of Christ Church at the early age of sixteen. Walton was able to study in the music library at Oxford, which contained scores by Stravinsky, Debussy, Ravel and others, and these opened up a new world to him.

When he was still only sixteen, he wrote the *Piano Quartet*, which is the first of his mature works. It was in Oxford that he met Roy Campbell, Ronald Firbank and Sacheverell Sitwell and formed a firm friendship with Sitwell, who brought down his brother Osbert to meet him. This was in 1919, and Osbert Sitwell has given this description of Walton at the time:

> The refinement of his rather long, narrow, delicately shaped head, and of his bird-like profile showing so plainly above the brow of the so-called bar or mound of Michelangelo that phrenologists claim to be the distinguishing mark of the artist – and especially of the musician – even his prominent, well-cut nose, scarcely gave a true impression either of his robust mental qualities or of the strength of his physique.

While at Oxford Walton worked only at music and virtually ignored other subjects; he therefore failed the official matriculation examination, and had to leave. There was talk at this time of sending him to one of the musical academies in London, but instead the Sitwells decided to look after him, and he lived with them for some time in London and Italy. The three Sitwells were then in the centre of the London artistic world, and they were able to introduce Walton to many aspects of art and to a number of people who could be of help to him.

Walton's first music to come before the international public was a string quartet, written in 1922 and played at the festival of the International Society for Contemporary Music held at Salzburg in 1923. This caused something of a scandal, for nobody in England had ever heard of Walton as a serious composer and did not even know whose pupil he was; moreover the work was atonal. Unfortunately it was placed at the end of a long programme and therefore did not make a great impression. Walton has since withdrawn it, but Alban Berg was interested by it, and took Walton to meet Schoenberg.

Shortly before this Walton had created another scandal with the first public performance of *Façade* on 12 June

1923 at the Aeolian Hall. This was devised by the Sitwells and Walton in collaboration, and was first performed privately in the Sitwells' London drawing-room in 1922. The title was taken from a remark by a bad painter who said of Edith Sitwell: 'Very clever, no doubt – but what is she but a façade?' Osbert Sitwell says: 'This had greatly delighted us, since what can any poet hope for better than to constitute a façade for his poetry? It seemed an admirable summing-up, and the very title for the sort of entertainment we wanted to present'. Walton had a series of long sessions with Edith Sitwell in which she read the words to him while he marked and accented them for his own guidance. It became necessary to amplify the words to balance the music: for this they discovered a machine called the Sengerphone, invented by a Swiss singer for the purpose of performing the part of Fafner, the dragon in Wagner's *Ring*.

The original scoring was for flute or piccolo, clarinet or bass clarinet, saxophone, trumpet, cello and percussion. The private performance of *Façade* in 1922 bewildered the Sitwells' friends, but this was nothing compared with the explosion caused by the public performance in 1923. Edith Sitwell wrote in her autobiography:

> The attitude of the audience was so threatening that I was warned to stay on the platform, hidden by the curtain, till they got tired of waiting for me and went home.

The critics described the music as 'collected from the works of the most eccentric of the ultra-moderns', while the words were dismissed as 'drivel'. In 1926 Walton revised the work and it was performed at the Siena meeting of the International Society for Contemporary Music; he later made two suites from the music for large orchestra, and these were subsequently made into a ballet by Frederick Ashton.

Walton was usually a slow worker, and his next important work was the *Sinfonia Concertante* for piano and orchestra, finished in 1927 and first performed at a Philharmonic concert under Ansermet on 5 January 1928, with York Bowen as soloist. This work is mainly in the neo-classical style, with some echoes of Stravinsky, though Walton's own voice can also be heard, especially in the central slow movement: the outer movements are brisker and more jazzy.

Before this he had written two slighter works, the overture *Portsmouth Point,* and *Siesta* for chamber orchestra. *Portsmouth Point* dates from 1925 and was prompted by a print by Thomas Rowlandson, the eighteenth-century caricaturist. The constantly changing accents and general sense of exhilaration in Walton's piece remind one of Stravinsky, but the feeling is English rather than continental. Walton's music in this period reacts against both romanticism and impressionism: it has perhaps more in common with the early chamber works of Hindemith than with any other music. Walton's characteristic vein of lyrical nostalgia has not yet appeared at this time, and *Façade* contains a good many parodies of popular music. *Siesta,* written in 1926, is for small orchestra, with some of the feeling of *Façade.*

Walton's next important work was the *Viola Concerto,* written in 1928–9. Beecham had suggested that Walton should write a viola concerto for Lionel Tertis; Walton sent the score to Tertis, who sent it back by return of post. But Edward Clark, in charge of modern music programmes at the BBC, suggested that Walton should send the score to Paul Hindemith, and it was Hindemith who played the solo part in the first performance at a Promenade concert on 3 October 1929, with the composer conducting. Tertis came to hear the work, was completely won over, and played the solo part in the International Festival of Contemporary Music at Liége the following year. In contrast with the classical feeling of the *Sinfonia Concertante*, the *Viola Concerto* is warm and lyrical; it is perhaps the first work in which Walton expresses the vein of nostalgia which he shares with Elgar and which is developed further in some of his later works.

The *Viola Concerto* had made Walton famous. Edward Clark suggested that he should be commissioned to write an oratorio for the next Leeds Festival in 1931; this was *Belshazzar's Feast,* probably the most striking English choral work of this century. The text was assembled by Osbert Sitwell, and combines the story of the fall of Babylon from the Book of Daniel with parts of Psalms 137 and 81, plus a passage from Revelation. As well as baritone soloist, mixed chorus and orchestra, Walton asked for two brass bands to be placed one on each side of the main orchestra; the effect of these in the barbaric chorus of praise to the heathen gods is shattering. There are also some fine lyrical passages in the work, especially in the opening section; the description of the writing on the wall is sung by the baritone soloist over a sinister percussion accompaniment.

During the next three years Walton was working on his *Symphony No. 1.* He was persuaded to allow the first three movements to be performed by the London Symphony Orchestra under Sir Hamilton Harty on 3 December 1934; the complete work was given its first performance on 6 November 1935 by the BBC Orchestra, again under Harty. The fact that the finale was not heard until later has made people think that it was tacked on afterwards, especially as it is somewhat different in style. But Walton himself has said that the coda of the finale was written at the same time as the slow movement. The passion of the slow movement makes the *Symphony No. 1* one of Walton's finest works, and with it he reached the climax of the first period of his career.

A violin concerto for Jascha Heifetz was completed in New York on 2 June 1939, and first performed in Cleveland on 7 December under the Polish conductor, Arthur Rodzinski. Heifetz reserved the right to perform it for two years. During the war, a precious copy of the solo part with Heifetz's markings was lost in the Atlantic. The first English performance was not until 1 November 1941, with Henry Holst as soloist.

Like Vaughan Williams, during the war Walton wrote a certain amount of music for films. He also transcribed some

Bach music, mostly from the cantatas, for the ballet *The Wise Virgins*; Walton's arrangements successfully avoid both archaism and ultra-modernity. He also wrote an original ballet, *The Quest*, based on a story from Spenser's *Faerie Queene*; this was first performed at the New Theatre in London in April 1943. It was not a success, probably because Walton had to write a forty-five-minute score in five weeks. As a result there was little chance for co-operation between the composer and the choreographer, Frederick Ashton; worse still, Robert Helpmann had to dance the part of St George in a white tunic and golden wig, which hardly suited his personality.

After the war, Walton returned to chamber music, a medium he had neglected for twenty years. In 1947 his *String Quartet* was first performed by the Blech Quartet. This is an attractive and lyrical work, and suits the instruments perfectly. It does not attempt to be heroic, nor does it contain the intimate thoughts of Beethoven's late quartets, but it is admirably written and the ideas are concisely and clearly expressed with Walton's usual nervous intensity.

In 1948 Walton attended an international conference in Buenos Aires where he met Señorita Susana Gil, whom he married the same year. The following year he wrote a *Violin Sonata* which was first performed in 1950 by Yehudi Menuhin and Louis Kentner; this again is largely a lyrical work. In the second movement, a set of variations, Walton introduces a twelve-note series but does not treat it in a Schoenbergian manner.

Walton's next major work was the opera *Troilus and Cressida*, produced at Covent Garden on 3 December 1954. The libretto was by Christopher Hassall, and was based on Chaucer rather than Shakespeare. It provided a carefully worked out dramatic plot and Walton wrote a highly romantic opera, in the sense that it looks back to the grand operas of the late nineteenth and early twentieth centuries, without however falling into pastiche. Walton is not afraid of strong and heroic gestures here, and in this opera he greatly enlarges his emotional range, though the music as such seems to present few new features. The opera enjoyed an immediate success. A shorter work composed in this period was the *Te Deum* for the coronation of Queen Elizabeth II on 2 June 1953: an extremely striking choral work and one of the best things Walton has done. It is concise and does not waste time; it has something of the immediacy and strength of *Belshazzar's Feast.* It is certainly very much more than an occasional piece. He wrote a coronation march, *Orb and Sceptre,* for the same ceremony.

The *Cello Concerto* written for Gregor Piatigorsky in 1956 begins, like the other concertos, with a slowish movement which is predominantly lyrical in style; the second movement is a rapid scherzo and the finale a set of variations. In 1958 came the *Partita,* commissioned by the Cleveland Orchestra; this is again one of Walton's 'public' works, with a brilliant first movement and finale, and a quieter slow movement.

1960 saw the *Symphony No. 2,* a slighter work than the first, though with many admirable features. In the finale of this work, a passacaglia, Walton again uses a twelve-note theme, as he did in the violin sonata, but he does not derive the harmonies from it. His most recent large orchestral work is the *Variations on a Theme by Hindemith,* the theme coming from Hindemith's *Cello Concerto.* This is a double tribute, both to Hindemith for undertaking the first performance of Walton's *Viola Concerto* so many years before, and to the Royal Philharmonic Society on the occasion of the hundred and fiftieth anniversary of its first concert.

Another recent work is *The Bear,* a short opera after Chekhov, first performed at the Aldeburgh Festival of 1967. A comic work, it includes a good deal of parody of other composers. Walton has also written a *Capriccio Burlesco* for orchestra for the 125th birthday of the New York Philharmonic Orchestra.

For some time now Walton has been living on the Mediterranean island of Ischia, where, as he puts it, he is 'creating and tending a large garden, a comparatively new and to me absorbing aspect of life'. He is no longer the *enfant terrible* of English music, and indeed even in his early days he never claimed to be an avant-garde composer. His more recent works, though no longer showing the violence of some of his thirties compositions, are written in a masterly manner.

Constant Lambert, slightly younger than Walton, was born in London on 23 August 1905. His father was the Australian painter G. W. Lambert, and his brother Maurice was a well-known sculptor; for this composer the visual arts were always as important as music. He was educated first at Christ's Hospital and later at the Royal College of Music, where he very early showed his brilliance, both as pianist and composer. In 1923 he met William Walton at the public performance of *Façade*. Both Walton and Lambert were greatly impressed by Peter Warlock. Apart from Warlock's flamboyant personality, Lambert was much influenced by his knowledge of Elizabethan music, from which he learnt a great deal; he did not, however, share Warlock's enthusiasm for Delius.

The first important musical event in Lambert's life was a request to write a ballet for Diaghilev, which was performed in 1926 at Monte Carlo when the composer was only twenty-one. The ballet was *Romeo and Juliet,* 'a rehearsal without scenery'. Lambert was furious with Diaghilev because he insisted on entrusting the decor to the Surrealist painters Ernst and Miró instead of to Lambert's friend, the young painter Christopher Wood. This resulted in a row with Diaghilev, but Lambert did write a second ballet for Nijinska, the choreographer of *Romeo and Juliet.* Its title was *Pomona,* and it was first performed at Buenos Aires in 1927. In both these ballets he used neo-classical forms deriving from the seventeenth and eighteenth centuries, rather than contemporary forms based on what he regarded as the 'smart-alec' techniques used by composers on the continent. Apart from classical dance forms, Lambert was interested in exotic music of various kinds, especially in jazz, and he dedicated his *Elegiac Blues* for small orchestra to Florence Mills. Jazz rhythms predominate in his *Piano Sonata* of 1929, and also in his most famous work, the *Rio Grande,* a setting of a poem by Sacheverell Sitwell for piano solo, chorus and orchestra. The work catches perfectly the sun-laden and sensual atmosphere of the poem.

A different kind of exoticism is found in the settings of eight poems of Li-Po for voice and a small group of instruments; these are charming and tender songs. Like Walton, Lambert reacted against both romanticism and impressionism, and though he did not follow the smart excesses of some contemporary French composers, his music definitely has its roots in a classical or pre-classical past.

By the age of twenty-five, Constant Lambert had achieved a commanding position in British music, equal to that of Walton. His life was far from easy, however; for a time he had to earn his living by playing music for ballet classes, which engendered in him a profound dislike for the marches and waltzes of Schubert used there for dancing practice. He had been undertaking more and more conducting work, and when, after the death of Diaghilev in 1929 and the disbanding of his company, the Camargo Society was started by Ninette de Valois and others, it was natural that Lambert, with his experience of ballet, should become its first conductor and musical director. This later became the Vic-Wells Ballet, which had little money at the time and consequently was unable to put on works for very large orchestra; but it enjoyed a good deal of support from the public, and also had some admirable dancers, including Alicia Markova, Anton Dolin, Robert Helpmann and the young Margot Fonteyn.

Lambert showed his interest in eighteenth-century music by editing eight symphonies and two overtures by William Boyce for modern performance. He was also a brilliant writer on music; in 1934, when still under thirty, he was asked to write a book on modern music and replied with *Music Ho!*, an excellent analysis of the trends of the twenties. Many people have disagreed with its conclusions; Lambert bitterly attacked Stravinsky, probably because of his associations with the Diaghilev Ballet, and, though appreciative of Schoenberg, he was inclined to think of him as too much of an academic figure. He emphasized the importance of the later works of Debussy and also of those of Satie, which are only really beginning to be appreciated in modern times. He also attacked the somewhat frivolous trends of some of the 'twenties' composers. The work also comments on a number of contemporary phenomena, including jazz, James Joyce and the Marx Brothers. After demolishing many of the gods of the day, Lambert put forward one figure whom he thought might lead to the future – Sibelius. He included a brief account of each of the Sibelius symphonies, believing them to hold the germ of a new symphonic form. We have seen now that he was not entirely right in this.

In 1936 Lambert wrote his most ambitious work, *Summer's Last Will and Testament,* described as a masque based on poems by Thomas Nashe (1593) for orchestra, solo baritone and chorus. This is cast in the dance and song forms of Nashe's period – madrigal, coranto, saraband and so on. It was Lambert's most deeply felt large-scale work, and it contains much fine music. The Scherzo, *King Pest,* is a brilliantly written piece for orchestra alone, and the final chorus is movingly nostalgic. The work is perhaps overlong, and there are some passages which are not up to the level of the finest moments in it. Unfortunately it was not a great success at its first performance given by the BBC in 1936, with the composer conducting. Although he was now only thirty-one, Lambert felt he was already a failure, and he wrote no more large-scale works, except for two ballets.

In 1936, Constant Lambert put on a Liszt ballet, *Apparitions,* at Sadler's Wells, with choreography by Frederick Ashton. For this he used the 'plot' of Berlioz's *Symphonie Fantastique,* and chose the music from the lesser-known works of Liszt; this was an enterprising procedure at the time, as Liszt was highly unpopular and most of his more interesting works were completely unknown. The ballet was a great success.

It was through Liszt that I first met Lambert. Sacheverell Sitwell's biography of Liszt had been published two years before, and reading it had made me very interested in him. As 1936 marked the fiftieth anniversary of Liszt's death, I decided to put on a Liszt concert in Oxford which would include some of his lesser-known works, among them the *Malediction* for piano and strings, a remarkable work which had never yet been performed publicly in England. I was a completely unknown undergraduate and wrote to Constant, who of course had never heard of me, asking if he would come and conduct a local orchestra in the *Malediction.* Although I was able to offer him only his expenses, he not only came and conducted the concert with great success, but wrote me several very helpful letters.

In 1937 Lambert wrote a new ballet for Sadler's Wells, *Horoscope,* based on the signs of the Zodiac; the choreography was again by Frederick Ashton. There were some striking passages, though it was not entirely original in ideas: some of the music has survived in the form of a suite. The palindrome which comes at the beginning of this ballet is a very curious piece, and quite unlike anything else that Constant wrote; he once told me that it had been dictated to him by Bernard van Dieren, who had died the previous year. Constant certainly believed in telepathic communication with other musicians (alive or dead) which indeed he often experienced.

During the war the Sadler's Wells Ballet toured a great deal, and Lambert of course went with them. One of their more interesting experiences was a visit to Holland in April 1940, when the company only just escaped from the approaching Germans. Lambert commemorated this in his *Aubade Héroïque* for orchestra, which expresses the atmosphere of the sunlit Dutch morning with the menace of war in the background. Another wartime work of Lambert's was the Dirge from *Cymbeline*, set for tenor and baritone soli, male chorus and strings; this is one of his most moving and beautiful works. It shows perhaps the influence of the chromatic harmony of Delius, but Shakespeare's words are expressed with great feeling; it is a short and concise work which certainly merits revival.

In 1944 Lambert conducted the first orchestral concert given by the Committee for the Promotion of New Music. He was always willing to take part in concerts of this kind, even if he did not always like the works to be performed; he was not a great admirer of avant-garde or twelve-tone music, but he respected it and was always willing to do his best for the composer, no matter what style he wrote in. Certain composers like Brahms he could not stand, and he was not very enthusiastic about folk-music, although he was a pupil of Vaughan Williams; in fact he once said, 'The only thing to be done with a folk tune after you had played it once was to play it again, louder'.

In the post-war years the Sadler's Wells Ballet moved to Covent Garden; Lambert went with them, but he did not get on very well with some of the opera authorities. In 1947 he resigned as chief conductor of the ballet, but he remained as its artistic adviser. He was also able to do a good deal of work for outside organizations. I had returned to a job at the BBC in 1946, and we collaborated on many programmes of unusual music for the Third Programme, which had begun in that year.

In the winter of 1946–7 Constant seemed to be wrapped in a perpetual gloom, the reason for which he would not disclose. However, in the spring of 1947 his spirits improved considerably, and shortly afterwards he met again Isabel Delmer, whom he had known for many years. They were married in September 1947. In the following year I managed to persuade him to write a work for piano duet for one of the concerts given by the London Contemporary Music Centre. This was the *Trois Pièces Nègres sur les Touches*

Blanches. As usual, he left the composition of this until the last moment, and it was not finished until April 1949, in Palermo, where he had gone to conduct at the festival of the ISCM. At the festival he got through the rehearsals only with the greatest of difficulty, but in the end achieved extremely good performances, and returned home in a much better state of health. On 17 May 1949 the *Trois Pièces Nègres* were performed for the first time, along with my setting of *Gold Coast Customs,* in which Constant and Edith Sitwell spoke the verse; he conducted Edith Sitwell in her part, and appeared to be conducting the conductor of the orchestra as well.

Lambert's last large work was the ballet *Tiresias,* produced at Covent Garden in July 1951 with choreography by Frederick Ashton and decor by Isabel Lambert. It was written for a rather unusual orchestra without upper strings, and unfortunately was not well received by the critics, in spite of magnificent performances by Margot Fonteyn and Michael Somes. This again made Constant very depressed. His health was not good at this time and he was liable to go into a coma for no apparent reason. One evening he called in Denis ApIvor to discuss a new ballet which ApIvor was to write for Covent Garden. Constant played ApIvor a recording of the *Waldteufel Waltz* that he had made, and seemed very happy and cheerful. But only a few hours later Denis ApIvor, who is a doctor as well as a composer, was summoned by Isabel because Constant was delirious. He had always refused to see doctors, and when he was rushed into hospital diabetes was diagnosed; but it was too late to save his life, and he died on 21 August 1951, two days before his forty-sixth birthday. At the memorial service for him the organ, on which Louis Kentner was to have played the *Aubade Héroïque,* suddenly failed for some unknown reason, and began to play again only after the service – it was an instrument that Constant had always loathed. At the opening concert of the Society for Twentieth-Century Music in Hampstead Town Hall in

January 1952, in which we played two of Constant's works, the *Li-Po* songs and his *Piano Concerto,* as a kind of memorial, another rather strange event occurred; at the beginning of the concert a large black cat appeared on the platform and remained there throughout the entire performance – after which it stalked off and was never seen again. Constant adored cats, and indeed once did a broadcast which began 'Cat, the friend of Man'.

Nowadays Lambert's music is not often played. But no one who met him could possibly forget him; Elisabeth Lutyens probably summed it up best when she said in a broadcast in 1965: 'I remember feeling that it isn't so much what he was or meant to us as a composer or a conductor, but it was the combination of his various activities, and, even more, I think, he was one of the most exciting, wide, generous personalities I have met. Music, London, living are duller without him'.

Two other British composers were typical of the twenties in different ways. Lord Berners (1883–1950) was a man of great versatility, not only a composer but also an admirable painter and author, and at one time a diplomat. He is chiefly remembered for his two ballets, *The Wedding Bouquet,* with words by Gertrude Stein and designs by himself – the speaking part was on many occasions recited by Constant Lambert – and *The Triumph of Neptune* which he wrote for Diaghilev, based on the old Victorian 'penny plain, tuppence coloured' prints. He wrote a number of works more or less in the contemporary French style which show a great deal of wit and irony. His music was mostly in the neo-classical tradition; clear, concise, with some use of parody: he normally avoided lyricism and nostalgia and in this way was working in parallel with composers such as Milhaud, Poulenc and Auric.

Eugene Goossens (1893–1962) was a very different composer. He came from an extremely musical family; his brother was Leon, the famous oboist, and his sisters Sidonie and Marie the well-known harpists. During the twenties he was one of the most brilliant of the younger conductors. He wrote two operas, *Judith* and *Don Juan de Mañara*, two symphonies and a good deal of chamber music; both his operas have libretti by Arnold Bennett. Writing somewhat in the French style – his family is of Belgian descent – he was acclaimed in the 1920s as one of the bright hopes of British music, but nowadays his works are rarely performed. His music has a solid character which is different from the 'debunking' style of his French contemporaries; it is possibly this heaviness in the writing which has made his music not wear so well as theirs.

4 British composers in the 1930s

Though the next group of British composers to appear on the scene were of approximately the same age as Walton and Lambert, they did not make their mark until much later, just before the Second World War. Two reasons for this were that most of the composers, including Berkeley, Tippett and Rawsthorne, developed rather late, and that feeling in this country was somewhat hostile towards modern music in general. When Edward Clark of the BBC invited Bartók to come over and play the solo part in his first two piano concertos, his music was received with incomprehension. The same applied to Webern, who was also invited by Clark to conduct works by Schoenberg and himself, as well as classical works. Berg's *Wozzeck* was given a concert performance by the BBC in 1934 under Sir Adrian Boult, and this provoked more appreciative reaction; but on the whole, the British public preferred to stick to more conservative paths.

Lennox Berkeley was born at Boar's Hill, near Oxford, on 12 May 1903; he was educated at a public school and Merton College, Oxford, going to Paris in 1927 to study with Nadia Boulanger for six years. He has said that at this period he felt great affinities with French composers and especially with Ravel. He admired the clarity, economy and restraint of most French music. Under Nadia Boulanger he studied counterpoint and fugue, and she helped him with his first attempts at composition; Berkeley admits to being greatly indebted to her. He also had an introduction to Ravel, who invited him to his house and looked at his works, though he did not then accept pupils. Berkeley says that Ravel insisted that meticulous care be given to the form and balance of a piece. He held the view that if one had something individual to say it would come out anyway, but that one must learn to say it as articulately and in as well-balanced a way as possible.

Berkeley's early works were naturally somewhat influenced by French models, but there was one rather interesting exception, the *Mont Juic Suite* for orchestra. Berkeley and Britten were together at the ISCM Festival in Barcelona in 1936, and in a park from which the suite takes its name they heard some folk-songs which Britten wrote down on pieces of paper and on the backs of envelopes. They decided to make a joint suite of these pieces, each writing two movements. Berkeley has said of this: 'It would only be possible for two composers who are fairly close to each other in style and outlook to do something like this successfully. Britten is the contemporary composer I have always been closest to in my own musical thinking and language'. But Berkeley went on to develop his own original style, characterized by clear textures, rhythmic ingenuity, an ability to make the most of slight material, a generally diatonic idiom and great practicality and neatness. This can be seen, for instance, in the oratorio *Jonah* of 1937, in the psalm *Domini est terra,* and especially in the *Serenade for Strings* of 1939 and in the *Divertimento in B flat* for small orchestra.

Berkeley's more recent works have shown his own individuality rather than the French style of his teacher. He has written three symphonies, of which the first, dating from 1940, made a great impression at a wartime Promenade concert; he has also written two piano concertos and a concerto for two pianos with orchestra. All these works show the clarity and restraint which he admires in French music, and they are entirely characteristic of Berkeley. His later works tend away from the diatonicism of the earlier ones: Berkeley has described his later style himself as 'harmonically less ordinary. It's not atonal of course; I can't express myself naturally in an atonal style.' And they certainly show more strength than the delightful but mainly slight pre-war works. Although he has said that he does not think of music in literary terms, he has done a good many settings. Some of these are of a religious nature, and include the *Stabat Mater* (1946), the *Four Poems of St Teresa of Avila* (1947) and *Ruth,* a short opera which can almost be described as a Theocritean idyll. Berkeley has written three other operas, of which the first, *A Dinner Engagement*, with a libretto by Paul Dehn, is extremely funny. The plot concerns an impoverished ex-ambassador and his wife who are entertaining to dinner the Grand Duchess of the country to which he was previously accredited and her son: there is a good deal of witty dialogue, mainly concerned with gastronomy, which the music turns into skilful parody. A large-scale work, *Nelson,* produced at Sadler's Wells in 1953, has not been entirely successful although it contains some striking and exciting scenes.

Berkeley's most recent opera, *The Castaway,* was produced at the Aldeburgh Festival of 1967, and is based on the Nausicaa episode from the *Odyssey,* again with a libretto by Paul Dehn. For some years Berkeley has lived in London and worked as a professor at the Royal Academy of Music. Apart from his larger works, he has written a number of smaller pieces, including some excellent piano music. In this he often resembles Poulenc, whose piano music showed him at his best: both composers have a fastidious approach which is often linked to irony or lyricism. He has always been a skilful and ingenious composer who has pursued his own path without worrying about fashion.

Michael Tippett was born in London on 2 January 1905 and spent his boyhood in Suffolk. His father was of Cornish stock and was originally a lawyer; through backing various successful enterprises, including the Lyceum Theatre in London, he was able to retire at a fairly early age. Tippett's mother was a writer, and was musical; from her he soon acquired a taste for music, and was given weekly piano lessons by the local village teacher. He continued his musical studies at Stamford Grammar School. In those days there was little opportunity for people living in the provinces to hear classical music, but at an early age Tippett heard Malcolm Sargent conducting a concert in Leicester which included Ravel's *Mother Goose Suite*, and this made a great impression on him.

After 1919 Tippett's parents lived mostly abroad, and he visited them on his holidays in France, Corsica or Florence. They were concerned about his wish to take up music as a career, but finally sent him to the Royal College of Music, where he studied composition with Charles Wood and conducting with Adrian Boult and Malcolm Sargent. In London he attended concerts and plays and took part in discussions about æsthetics, ethics, politics, religion and any other subject which excited young people at that time. He used to go to the Promenade concerts every night, and here got to know the Beethoven symphonies; he had previously studied the piano sonatas when living in the provinces. Beethoven remained the composer he most admired, though later he felt attracted by Palestrina, the Elizabethans, Purcell, Handel, and modern composers such as Bartók, Hindemith and Stravinsky.

On leaving the College he taught French for two or three years at a school in Surrey. However as he had a small private income he was able to give up teaching, and built a cottage near Oxted, where he was invited to be the conductor of the local choral society. There he put on a number of operatic productions, including works by Vaughan Williams and Stanford; he also adapted an eighteenth-century ballad opera, *The Village Opera*, of which he rewrote one act. A concert of his works was given in Oxted in 1930, conducted by David Moule-Evans; as a result of this, Tippett decided to scrap most of what he had written. The works included a *Concerto in D* for flutes, oboes, horns and strings, which he destroyed, a string quartet in F and a psalm in C for chorus and orchestra. Deciding that his technique was immature, he arranged to study counterpoint privately with R. O. Morris for eighteen months. Even so, works written after this period – a *Symphony in B flat* and a *Song of Liberty* for chorus – were also eventually discarded; but others remain well-known today; among them the *String Quartet No. 1* of 1935, the *Piano Sonata No. 1* of 1937, and the *Double Concerto for String Orchestra* of 1939, which is one of his most performed works. This has been described by Tippett himself as 'a study in polyphony', and it shows a combination of various strands in different rhythms; Tippett has always been interested in the metrical irregularities of Elizabethan music and has often combined these with a more modern idiom. He has said of himself, 'I am a born contrapuntalist and feel the polyphonic line very much in my bones'.

During this period, Tippett also became conductor of the South London Orchestra, which consisted mainly of unemployed professional musicians who had lost their jobs in cinema bands when talking films arrived. He wrote and arranged music for performances by schoolchildren, as well as a folk-song opera, *Robin Hood,* for a group of Yorkshire miners. The South London Orchestra rehearsed regularly at Morley College and gave concerts in London County Council schools. Tippett was already playing a large part in the musical activities of Morley College, and when the war started he was called on to take a greater measure of responsibility for it. On 15 October 1940 the building sustained a direct hit by a bomb, but classes went on at a neighbouring school, and Tippett was appointed director of music in succession to Arnold Foster. At Morley College he raised the musical standard considerably, building up the choir from eight voices to thirty. The concerts had to be given in the small Holst Room which held only a hundred and fifty people. Most wartime concerts consisted of the familiar classics, but Tippett was able to put on Monteverdi, the Elizabethans, a great deal of Purcell, the Bach family, and modern composers such as Debussy, Stravinsky and Hindemith. He also started recorder classes at the College, and edited a number of early works in conjunction with Walter Bergmann.

Meanwhile he had begun writing a large work, the oratorio *A Child of Our Time*, suggested by an incident in Paris in 1938; a young Polish Jew had shot a German diplomat in revenge for the persecution his mother had suffered at the hands of the Nazis. This incident had led to a pogrom of the Jews throughout Central Europe, and Tippett planned his work as a protest. Deciding to cast it as an oratorio rather than as an opera, he approached T. S. Eliot, who had recently written *The Family Reunion,* to ask whether he would be interested in collaborating. Tippett showed Eliot a rough draft, and Eliot replied that Tippett had already done the job himself, and that there was no need for him to intervene. So Tippett wrote his own libretto, beginning the work two days after the outbreak of war and completing it in 1943.

A Child of Our Time uses negro spirituals in the manner of Bach chorales to comment on the story and intersperse the dramatic sections: this mixture of styles makes the work somewhat uneven, though it contains many moving moments arising out of the tragic story. While working on it, Tippett met Benjamin Britten and Peter Pears, recently returned from America, and in January 1943 wrote a vocal cantata for them, *Boyhood's End,* with words by W. H. Hudson; it was performed early in the summer of 1943 in the Holst Room at Morley College. This work is on the lines of the Purcell solo cantatas, with considerable use of melismata in the vocal line, great rhythmical freedom and an original use of a diatonic idiom. In the autumn of 1942 Tippett had appeared before a tribunal in London, stating his conscientious objections to active war service, and had been exempted on the condition that he take up some approved work such as agriculture or hospital work. He refused because he was convinced that music was the field with which he could best serve the community, and he was eventually tried at Oxted. In spite of Vaughan Williams's intervention on his behalf, he was sentenced to three months' imprisonment in the summer of 1943. Tippett's mother had been a suffragette, and she said in later years: 'My proudest moment was the day when he went to prison'.

On returning to Morley College, Tippett continued with his monthly concerts; about this time Britten asked him if he had written any larger works and was shown the score of *A Child of Our Time.* He suggested that it be performed as soon as possible, and its first performance took place on 19 March 1944, conducted by Walter Goehr. It made a considerable impact. When the war ended Tippett and Goehr set up the Morley College Concert Society with financial backing from the Arts Council, and played a number of old and new works of different kinds. These included Monteverdi's *Vespers* of 1610, Stravinsky's *Les Noces,* the first performance of Seiber's *Ulysses* and the first London performance of Tippett's *Symphony No. 1* of 1947.

Tippett retired as director of music at Morley College in 1951. His works continued to gain more and more favourable criticism. In 1946 he had begun his first full-scale opera, *The Midsummer Marriage.* He first wrote the libretto of each act and then the music. This took him six years, and it was completed in October 1952. It was first performed at Covent Garden on 27 January 1955. At this time the main criticisms were of the libretto, which has been described as a modern version of the *Magic Flute.* The music, however, was genuinely appreciated, and a recent revival of it at Covent Garden has earned it even greater praise. The orchestral writing is mainly polyphonic, and varies from strong rhythmical invention, as in the choral finale of the first act, to the simplicity of Sosostris' aria in the third; there are many lyrical passages of great beauty, and the style is in some ways reminiscent of Walton's earlier works. Tippett made an orchestral suite of the four *Ritual Dances* from it, which has been frequently played in orchestral concerts. His shorter works include a second string quartet (1941–2), a revised version of the first string quartet (1943), a third quartet (1946), *Little Music for String Orchestra* (also 1946) and a song cycle, *The Heart's Assurance* (1951) based on poems by Sidney Keyes and Alun Lewis, who were both killed in the Second World War. This was first performed by Pears and Britten in May 1951.

Since the end of the war Tippett has given a number of broadcast talks, and after the death of Schoenberg in 1951 he contributed a series of talks called *Moving into Aquarius.* These were subsequently published in a book, which also included another series called *The Birth of an Opera,* about the genesis of *The Midsummer Marriage.* Tippett has made a number of appearances on television, and taken part in broadcast and televised discussions, not always on musical subjects. He has said that his thinking has been profoundly influenced by Goethe, Jung, Shaw and Brecht. He was present at the first productions of many of Shaw's plays, when Shaw was at his most brilliant, and he particularly appreciated Shaw's ability to mock intellectual nonsense. He was also intrigued by Brecht's ideas on the epic theatre, which attracted him when he was writing his second opera, *King Priam.* He regards Goethe as a genius equal to Beethoven.

After *The Midsummer Marriage* Tippett wrote a *Fantasia Concertante* on a theme of Corelli for string orchestra, commissioned by the Edinburgh Festival of 1953. In the same year Benjamin Britten invited six composers (Berkeley, Britten, Oldham, Tippett, Walton and myself) to write a variation for string orchestra on the Elizabethan tune *Sellinger's Round* for the Aldeburgh Festival. Tippett wrote a slow variation for this and in the following year expanded it into a *Divertimento* for chamber orchestra, in response to a commision from Paul Sacher, the Swiss conductor. In 1955 a piano concerto was commissioned by the City of Birmingham Symphony Orchestra; this was not an enormous success because of the very complex writing for both soloist and orchestra, but it has won greater appreciation since its first performance. The *Symphony No. 2* commissioned by the BBC, was first performed by Sir Adrian Boult and the BBC Symphony Orchestra in February 1958. This work shows a greater clarity than the *Symphony No. 1* which was not altogether a success, and has some interesting sonorities and an original use of texture; though somewhat reminiscent of Stravinsky, the texture is handled by Tippett in an extremely individual way.

In the summer of 1957 Tippett was offered a commission by the Koussevitzky Music Foundation to write a choral and orchestral work. He accepted this, but on starting the composition found it could be better expressed in the form of an opera, which in due course became his second opera, *King Priam.* Again Tippett wrote his own libretto, this time basing it on scenes from the Iliad. The opera was written between 1958 and 1961, and first performed at Covent Garden in 1962. Tippett says of it that it makes 'certain dramatic gestures. This work is therefore technically nearer the Russian Impressionist style'. In it he breaks down the orchestra into small groups of instruments. The whole orchestra very rarely appears together, and the strings are seldom used all at once, but combine with other groups of instruments; there are no strings at all in the second act, and the piano, which has an important part, is often used in conjunction with other instruments, such as trombones. *King Priam* is clearer, both in plot and music, than *The Midsummer Marriage,* and has recently been revived with success. Motifs from *King Priam* appear in several later works, including the *Piano Sonata No. 2* of 1962 and the *Concerto for Orchestra,* completed in 1963 and dedicated to Benjamin Britten on his fiftieth birthday. In the *Concerto for Orchestra* the ensemble is again divided into several small groups used antiphonally, often with new and remarkable sound combinations. The texture is much more transparent than in many of Tippett's earlier works, and there is again an original, if sometimes Stravinskian use of sonorities. A more recent large-scale work, the cantata *The Vision of St Augustine* of 1965, goes further in this direction, and has an added dramatic emphasis which makes it one of the most successful of Tippett's works. Tippett's third opera, *The Knot Garden,* was first produced at Covent Garden in December 1970. The libretto has something in common with that of *The Midsummer Marriage,* both being concerned with spiritual quests, but *The Knot Garden* is about life in the modern world, including such with-it characters as a woman freedom fighter and a homosexual male couple, one of them a Negro. The music, much terser and more varied than that of the previous operas, contains many striking effects, and is partly based on a twelve-note row; blues and other elements of pop music also appear. The dialogue is not without its banalities; the third act contains charades on themes from *The Tempest.*

Tippett lived for a long time at Wadhurst in Sussex, but in 1960 moved to Wiltshire, where he still lives. In 1959 he was made a CBE and in 1964 given an Honorary Doctorate of Music at Cambridge. He was knighted in 1965. He is generally regarded as one of the most important British composers of our time. Because he works slowly and because each major work presents new ideas, it is very difficult to say how he will develop in the future; at least we know that something original and interesting will emerge.

Alan Rawsthorne was born in Haslingden, Lancashire, on 2 May 1905. He trained originally to be a dentist, as his parents were opposed to the idea of a musical career for him. Eventually he managed to persuade them, and he entered the Royal Manchester College of Music in 1926. He won prizes in his two main subjects – piano and composition – and took his college diploma in 1929. He then went abroad, where he studied piano with Egon Petri. Although an excellent pianist, he never wished to become a virtuoso, and on his return to England took a post at Dartington Hall, where he taught and provided music for the school of dance mime from 1932 to 1934. In 1934 he married Jessie Hinchcliffe, a violinist and a fellow-student at the Manchester College of Music. She soon obtained a position in the newly formed BBC Symphony Orchestra and in 1934 the Rawsthornes settled in London.

The earliest works which Rawsthorne has preserved date from this period. They include a *Concertante for Violin and Piano*, a *Sonata for Viola and Piano* and a *Concerto for Clarinet and String Orchestra.* Rawsthorne's first really mature work was the *Theme and Variations for Two Violins* of 1937; it was performed at the 1938 London Festival of the International Society for Contemporary Music, and the international public at once realized that here was a new composer who had something significant and relevant to say. Rawsthorne showed great originality and ingenuity in handling this difficult and limited medium. He had by now developed a freely atonal style, to some extent based on false relations, a style which he was to use for twenty years or more; every bar of his music is unmistakably Rawsthorne. The *Variations* were followed in 1939 by a larger work, the *Symphonic Studies* for orchestra. This again uses a kind of variation form, but in a much broader manner, and it contains dramatic and lyrical passages as well as a dry humour and wit which are characteristic of all Rawsthorne's works. His *String Quartet No. 1*, also in the form of variations, dates from 1939, as does the original version of his *Piano Concerto No. 1* which was at this time orchestrated for strings and percussion only; in 1942 Rawsthorne revised the work and rescored it for full orchestra. Its slow movement is again a set of variations, this time in the form of a chaconne.

In 1941 Rawsthorne joined the army, and after brief experience as a gunner entered the Army Educational Corps, where he was one of the few composers to hold the exalted rank of Sergeant-Major. He naturally had little time for composition, but was able to write an *Ode to the Red Army* in 1942, and *Street Corner,* an overture commissioned by ENSA which shows his rather cheeky brand of wit at its best.

After the war he was able to return to composition in a more regular manner, and his first work to attract attention was the fantasy overture *Cortèges.* In the composer's words, this 'is constructed out of musical elements of a processional character, veering from a funeral march to a lively tune in light infantry tempo'.

One of Rawsthorne's most successful works, the *Concerto for String Orchestra,* was first performed on the Hilversum radio in 1949 and in London in the same year. His first symphony followed in 1950. Another extremely successful work, the *Piano Concerto No. 2,* was commissioned for the Festival of Britain in 1951, and since then has been played all over the world. These works are a continuation and summing up of his previous work rather than a new departure; the *Concerto for String Orchestra* has been described as 'a work in a line from the Elgar *Introduction and Allegro* to the Tippett *Double Concerto*'. The first symphony is violent, harsh and aggressive; the second piano concerto is more lyrical and contains many witty passages, especially in the finale.

Not long after this Rawsthorne went to live in a village in Essex. His first marriage had been dissolved, and in 1954 he married Isabel, the widow of Constant Lambert. The second violin concerto followed in 1956.

Rawsthorne's next major work was the *Symphony No. 2* of 1959; subtitled *The Pastoral Symphony,* it has a soprano solo in the last movement. It is rather slighter and quieter than many of his previous works. Shortly after this Rawsthorne's style began to change; it became more chromatic, more concentrated, and less dependent on certain harmonic formulae which he had developed even in his prewar works. This new style can be seen in the *Mediæval Diptych* for baritone solo and orchestra, produced in London in 1962, as well as in the *Symphony No. 3* one of his most important works, and in the third string quartet. The symphony has a dark, mysterious character, often 'vehement and impassioned' as the composer describes it himself, but with reflective passages as well; the second movement is a Sarabande and the third is a hushed Scherzo. The finale is more extrovert and contains a theme which the composer describes as 'obstreperous, emphatic and a little vulgar in essence', but the work ends quietly. Other important works of this period were the *Carmen Vitale* for soprano solo, mixed chorus and orchestra, and the *Cello Concerto* of 1966.

Rawsthorne's later works included a *Theme, Variations and Finale* for a school orchestra at Chelmsford, written in 1967, providing brilliant music, exciting to play and yet in no way 'written down' to young players. He commemorated the death of his friend and colleague, Louis MacNeice, with a very moving *Elegiac Rhapsody* for string orchestra. His last works were a short but effective *Quintet for Piano and Strings* and a *Concerto for Two Pianos and Orchestra.*

After he moved to the country Rawsthorne's life was comparatively uneventful. He did not teach, rarely wrote or lectured about music and conducted only his own works. I feel that his contribution to English music is as important as that of any composer working in England today, and that this will be realized more and more as time goes by. He died on 24 July 1971.

5 Benjamin Britten

Benjamin Britten, the best-known English composer of today, was born at Lowestoft, Norfolk, on 22 November 1913 – the feast day of St Cecilia, patron saint of music. His mother was an amateur musician who enjoyed singing, and musical evenings took place in the Britten household. Distinguished soloists often came down to take part in these performances, so that Benjamin Britten was familiar with musicians from a very early age. Britten's father was not a musician – he was a dentist – but he enjoyed music, and felt strongly enough about it not to want to have a wireless set or gramophone in the house, as he thought it might prevent people from making their own music.

Britten started writing music at the age of five; at first he simply drew patterns on paper, but later he composed 'tone poems' for piano lasting twenty seconds. His mother gave him his first piano lessons and at the age of eight he was taught by a local school-teacher. Soon he was able to accompany his mother's songs and play duets with the organist of the local church. He was good at his lessons, particularly mathematics, at his preparatory school in Lowestoft and the headmaster hoped that he would win a scholarship to a public school. He still managed to find time for composition, and an extraordinary number of songs and instrumental pieces date from this period.

Apart from the piano he learned the viola, and his string

pieces give every detail of bowing. Similarly, the piano pieces contain pedal marks and the organ pieces registration directions. Britten had been given Stainer's *Rudiments* for his ninth birthday, and from then on covered his pieces with Italian directions. He began taking harmony lessons when he was ten, but he was familiar with very few twentieth-century works. When he was twelve he wrote an overture in B flat minor for full orchestra which was ninety-one pages long. By now his parents realized that he would need an experienced teacher.

Fortunately Frank Bridge came to East Anglia at about this time. Britten was taken to see him, and after this he went to him regularly, either to Eastbourne or London; he was grateful to Bridge for his strictness and professionalism. Up to the time he was thirteen or fourteen he had written mostly in an early nineteenth-century style, but after hearing Holst's *Planets* and Ravel's *String Quartet*, he started using a freer harmonic idiom, which Bridge tended to disapprove of. Britten also studied Bridge's own music; at that time Bridge was turning from his earlier romantic style to the almost atonal period of his last years.

From 1928 to 1930 Britten was at Gresham's School in Holt, Norfolk, where the music master greeted him with the words: 'So you are the little boy who likes Stravinsky'. His musical training at Gresham's he described later as 'practically non-existent'. But there was a school choir and orchestra, and chamber concerts were given.

In 1930 Britten went to the Royal College of Music, and at Frank Bridge's suggestion studied with John Ireland. Apart from the dictation class, in which he was outstanding, Britten visited the College only for his weekly composition lessons. The scarcity of contemporary music in the College library disturbed him, but when he asked that a score of Schoenberg's *Pierrot Lunaire* be added to the library, the request was turned down. By this time he was breaking away from his earlier love of nineteenth-century German music, having discovered Purcell and the English madrigalists. To some extent, he was reacting against the influence of Frank Bridge, whose background was mostly eighteenth- and nineteenth-century German.

In Britten's last year at the College he was given a small travelling scholarship, and wanted to go to Vienna to study with Berg, whom Bridge greatly admired. However, the authorities frustrated his plans.

By this time Britten had already written the first work which was to make him known, *A Boy was Born,* a set of variations for unaccompanied chorus, composed in the winter of 1932–3. This is an astonishing work for a composer of his age, full of ideas and imaginative sounds; to some extent it was awkwardly written for the voices, as Britten had not attended the choral class at the College and did not have a very clear idea of what the human voice could do. Twenty years later Britten revised the work and simplified it.

On leaving the college at the age of nineteen Britten had to earn his living, and he managed to make contact with a documentary film company. This company had very little money, and Britten had to write scores for not more than six or seven players; instead of using sound effects, they had to imitate natural sounds by various means. In the film *Night Mail,* written for the Post Office Film Unit, the sound of a train approaching through a tunnel was required. Britten recorded a cymbal clash, then reversed it so that the vibrations increased and cut off the actual clash. This anticipated the *musique concrète* of the 1940s. The script of *Night Mail* was by W. H. Auden, who had been at Gresham's School some years before Britten. Britten collaborated with Auden not only in films but by writing incidental music for plays; at the Group Theatre he also collaborated with Isherwood and others.

In 1934 he was asked to write a book of songs for a boys' school where his brother was headmaster; the result was *Friday Afternoons,* a set of twelve children's songs with piano. In the same year Britten's *Suite for Violin and Piano* was played at the Barcelona Festival of the ISCM, and in

10 Lennox Berkeley (b. 1903) (left) rehearsing with Yehudi Menuhin at the 1961 Bath Festival.

11 Constant Lambert (1905–1951) was a brilliant figure in London's twenties, but wrote less as he grew older. Here he rehearses the Covent Garden Orchestra in the Chabrier ballet *Ballabile* (1950).

12 Benjamin Britten (b. 1913), England's best-known living composer (left) a
E. M. Forster, with whom he collaborated on the opera *Billy Budd* (1951).

13 Britten (left) and the Russian pianist Sviatoslav Richter rehearsing Mozart at Blythburgh.

14 Britten in front of the burnt-out concert hall at the Maltings, Snape (6 June 1969).

15 Michael Tippett (b. 1905) is an outstanding individual force as composer, conductor and teacher. Here he instructs at a school for rural conductors (1948).

16 Alan Rawsthorne (1905–1971) (right) with a pupil at the Bryanston Music School.

the following year his *Variations on a Theme of Frank Bridge* for string orchestra was played at the Salzburg Festival. *Friday Afternoons* is an early example of Britten's remarkable gift for achieving original results by very simple methods; the *Violin Suite* is ingenious and concentrated, and says a good deal in a short space. The *Frank Bridge Variations* show Britten's mastery of several different styles and contain a great variety of moods.

He had produced an amusing suite of arrangements of Rossini's *Soirées Musicales* in 1936, and in 1938 he wrote his *First Piano Concerto,* performing the solo part in it himself at a Promenade concert. In 1939 he wrote a choral work, *Ballad of Heroes,* to poems by W. H. Auden and Randall Swingler; this was written for a Festival of Music for the People, given in April 1939 in memory of Britons who fell in the Spanish Civil War, fighting on the Republican side. One of its features is the placing of trumpets away from the main orchestra in the gallery. Britten also wrote a companion work, *Advance Democracy,* again with words by Randall Swingler. But he was beginning to feel somewhat disillusioned with the lack of work in England, and his friend W. H. Auden had gone to America. Britten's parents had both died; the house in Lowestoft had been sold. He felt rather rootless and decided to try his luck in America; he sailed there early in 1939.

He found America 'enormously stimulating'. He spent six months in Brooklyn and then settled in Long Island. Among his American works are the *Violin Concerto,* written for the Spanish violinist Antonio Brosa, *Diversions* for piano left hand and orchestra for the one-armed Viennese pianist Paul Wittgenstein, as well as his *First String Quartet*. Meanwhile, the tenor Peter Pears had come to America in 1939. Britten wrote *The Seven Sonnets of Michelangelo* for tenor and piano for Pears to sing, and the two of them began a partnership which has lasted till this day, with recitals all over the world.

The *Michelangelo Sonnets* are written in a broad Italianate style which is highly suitable to the words, though there is no question of a pastiche of Italian music: they are a good example of Britten's original use of diatonic methods.

Auden had by now become an American citizen; although Britten was considering the same step, he had become increasingly homesick in the States. While in California he had seen an article by E. M. Forster on the poet George Crabbe who lived and worked in Suffolk. 'To talk about Crabbe (wrote Forster) is to talk about England. He did not go to London much, but lived in villages and small country towns. He was born at Aldeburgh on the coast of Suffolk. Nearby is a quay, at the side of an estuary, and here the scenery becomes melancholy and flat; expanses of mud, saltish commons, the marsh birds crying. Crabbe heard that sound and saw that melancholy, and it got into his verse'. Britten had known that Suffolk country all his life, and reading this article he determined to return to England as soon as possible; meanwhile he bought a copy of Crabbe's poems and read *The Borough.* From this reading came the idea for the opera *Peter Grimes.*

Britten and Pears returned to England in 1942. They brought with them several new pieces, including *Les Illuminations,* a song cycle of settings of poems by Rimbaud for voice and string orchestra; also an unaccompanied choral piece, *Hymn to St Cecilia,* with words by W. H. Auden, and *A Ceremony of Carols* for high voices and harp. *Les Illuminations* provided ingenious settings of Rimbaud's prose poems which bring out the spirit of the words without being directly pictorial; the fusion of words and music has a quasi-surrealist effect in keeping with the poems. Both convinced pacifists, Britten and Pears had to appear before a tribunal; they were granted exemption from war service on condition that they continued to give song recitals all over England.

Besides performing, Britten was able to compose during the remaining years of the war. In 1943 he wrote one of his best-known works, the *Serenade* for tenor, horn and strings, settings of poems which range from an anonymous dirge of the fifteenth century to Jonson, Keats and Tennyson. He also made many arrangements of British folk-songs.

When in London, Britten usually stayed with Erwin Stein, who had been a pupil of Schoenberg in Vienna and had known Mahler; he helped and encouraged Britten until his death in 1958. When in the country, Britten went down to the mill at Snape, where his sister was living with her children, and there he was able to work on *Peter Grimes.* He worked on it all through 1944, and by the beginning of 1945 it was finished.

Though opera was in a parlous state in England during the war, the first performance of *Peter Grimes* was given at Sadler's Wells on 7 June 1945, a month after the end of the war in Europe. It was a triumph. In this highly dramatic work Britten's chief concern is to display the voices of the protagonists, minor characters and chorus, while the orchestra plays a subordinate part, except in the six interludes. The gulf between Peter Grimes, a 'maladjusted aggressive psychopath', as he has been described, and the rest of the world is suggested by a fragmentary style of utterance and by the use of intervals larger than an octave, sometimes also by bitonality. In this opera, which Britten regards as his most realistic, he was able to delineate complex psychological states of mind. It has remained an eminently successful work.

Two months later, in August 1945, Britten toured the concentration camps of Germany with Yehudi Menuhin, giving two or three short recitals a day; the impact this had on him made him 'defy the nightmare horror' by writing his *Holy Sonnets of John Donne*, in which death is triumphantly defeated. These use musical conceits which recall the fanciful and unorthodox side of Purcell; the last sonnet, 'Death be not proud' on a firm ground bass has been described as 'both simple and fanciful, sensuous and austere'. This song cycle was first performed by Britten and Pears on St Cecilia's Day 1945; the previous day Britten had heard the first performance of his *Second String Quartet,* written, like the Sonnets, for the two hundred and fiftieth anniversary of the death of Purcell – a composer with whom Britten has always been in sympathy. The last movement of this quartet is a strongly Purcellian passacaglia. Britten used one of Purcell's themes for the variations known as *The Young Person's Guide to the Orchestra.*

Britten now began considering a further opera. Eric Crozier suggested the rape of Lucretia as a theme; Ronald Duncan worked out a libretto with Britten. Kathleen Ferrier, then completely unknown, was found ideal for the part of Lucretia, and it became her first operatic appearance. Tippett too was interested in this theme, and even wanted to set it as well, on the precedent of many eighteenth-century operas when the same libretti were used by different composers; but Britten was not happy about this, and the idea came to nothing.

Lucretia was first performed at Glyndebourne in the summer of 1946; in contrast with *Peter Grimes,* which has a large cast and a full orchestra. *Lucretia* has only eight singers and a small chamber orchestra. The conflict between Tarquin and Lucretia, representing the forces of evil and good respectively, is shown musically by the use of two versions of the diminished fourth B natural – E flat. Tarquin is represented by a descending scale, Lucretia by two thirds in contrary motion. These two motifs are used in many permutations. The Christian element in a Roman story somewhat bewildered listeners; Britten wrote to a friend: 'I used to think the day when you could shock people was over – but now I have discovered that being simple, and considering things spiritual of importance, produces violent reactions!'

After *Lucretia,* Britten wanted to write a comedy and eventually decided on *Albert Herring,* adapted by Eric Crozier from Maupassant's story *Le Rosier de Madame Husson.* He transplanted this very Gallic story into an East Anglian setting, so that a good deal of the French wit and atmosphere disappeared. Nevertheless, *Albert Herring* was a success following its production in 1947. The music is 'light and loose, mercurial and full of fun'; Britten uses the 'love potion' theme from *Tristan* at the point where Albert's lemonade is laced with rum to start him off on his spree. The opera contains a number of free recitatives in which each part goes on its own way without regard for the others.

Soon after the first performance of *Albert Herring*, Britten gave up the mill at Snape and went to live in Aldeburgh. In August 1947 Peter Pears suggested to Britten that they should start their own festival at Aldeburgh. The first festival was held in 1948, beginning in Aldeburgh Church with a performance of Britten's cantata *St Nicholaos,* sung by a choir of a hundred singers from East Suffolk. For the following year Britten wrote a short children's opera called *The Little Sweep* or *Let's Make an Opera,* again with words by Eric Crozier. This, too, was set in Suffolk, and members of the audience were invited to join in some of the songs. The Aldeburgh Festival, now in its twenty-fourth year, has continued to grow with the town, and besides Britten's latest works, it has included a number of first performances of works by other composers such as Tippett, Walton, Berkeley, Gerhard and Henze.

In 1948 Britten began to work on the *Spring Symphony*, a choral symphony in four movements based on fourteen poems relating to spring, dating from the fourteenth to the seventeenth centuries. Here Britten shows great skill in setting heterogeneous material and still making it into a symphony rather than a suite.

Two years later came another large-scale opera, *Billy Budd*, which had been commissioned for the Festival of Britain. *Billy Budd* was based on a short novel by the American writer Herman Melville, and the opera used only men's voices. It was first performed at Covent Garden in 1951. *Billy Budd* was a success with the public, if not always with the critics.

In 1953 Britten was asked to write an opera in honour of

the coronation of Queen Elizabeth II and chose *Gloriana* with a libretto by William Plomer after Lytton Strachey's *Elizabeth and Essex. Gloriana* was produced on 8 June 1953 at Covent Garden in the presence of the Queen and the whole court. It was perhaps a mistake to have made this occasion so official; some exception was taken to the libretto, which in places showed one of the Queen's ancestors in a somewhat unfavourable light, and the music was incomprehensible to a good many of the audience. *Gloriana* was, in fact, judged a failure at the time, though it has since been revived with considerable success. Each of the eight scenes is complete in itself and has an orchestral prelude. The opera lacks the cumulative musical flow of some of Britten's other operas, such as *Peter Grimes, The Rape of Lucretia* and *The Turn of the Screw*, but it contains some vivid self-contained tableaux, and Queen Elizabeth herself is imaginatively presented.

Britten soon recovered from this near-disaster, and his next opera, *The Turn of the Screw*, is one of his best and most ingenious works. Based on the Henry James story, it is another chamber opera: between the scenes it contains sixteen orchestral interludes which are in fact a theme and fifteen variations on a fairly simple twelve-note row, a series of ascending fifths used tonally, not serially. The supernatural elements in the opera are identified with flat keys and flattened notes; at the end the white-note keys triumph over the black-note ones. There is a skilful use of atmosphere: one scene, for instance, is dominated by church bells and another by the piano, which plays what amounts to a miniature piano concerto.

Along with these large works Britten continued to compose smaller ones, including three canticles and two song cycles, *A Charm of Lullabies* (1947) and *Winter Words*, eight settings of Thomas Hardy, written in 1953.

Britten's major work of that period was a ballet in three acts, *The Prince of the Pagodas*, which was performed at Covent Garden in 1957 with choreography by John Cranko.

Britten's voyage to the Far East in 1955 had introduced him to oriental music and he incorporated many Eastern effects into the score, especially in the scene of the pagodas, which has an elaborate percussion part. The score contains about thirty-six dances, and Britten was successful in defining and diversifying the different rhythmical shapes of the tunes used in each. Original and striking musically, it was rather too long dramatically, with two divertissements, one in the second and one in the third act, which held up the action.

Noye's Fludde, a setting of the Chester Miracle Play, was written for the Aldeburgh Festival of 1958. This again is a work written for performance partly by amateurs and partly by professionals; the professionals provide a solo string quartet, treble recorder, piano duet, organ and timpani, while children play strings and recorders, bugles, handbells and percussion, and of course also sing. The story of the flood is told in simple language, and with ingenious use of Anglican hymns.

In 1959 Britten wrote a *Missa Brevis* for the organist and choristers of Westminster Catholic Cathedral, a highly original setting of the Mass. In 1960 came one of his finest works, the opera *A Midsummer Night's Dream,* based on Shakespeare. It is scored for a large chamber ensemble, but has been successfully produced in large opera houses. The fairies are characterized by harps, harpsichord, celesta and percussion – Britten says: 'I have always been struck by a kind of sharpness in Shakespeare's fairies' – and they were originally played by boys, not girls; the lovers are portrayed by woodwind and strings, and the mechanicals by the lower brass and bassoon. The opening string glissandi give the feeling of the slumbering wood; the fairies' music is tart rather than pretty. The mechanicals' play satirises nineteenth-century romantic opera. *A Midsummer Night's Dream* succeeds through its differentiation between the natural and supernatural worlds and its characterization of different groups of persons.

In the same year he wrote his *Cantata Academica* for the

University of Basle in Switzerland, to a sequence of Latin texts; employing various traditional techniques, such as canon and fugue, ostinato bass, chorales, arias, duets and recitatives, and even a note-row. Though the latter is hardly used in a Schoenbergian manner, it does appear as a fugue subject in the eighth movement of the cantata; Britten had also used note-rows in a fairly simplified manner in *The Turn of the Screw* and *A Midsummer Night's Dream.*

Britten's most famous work of recent years is his *War Requiem,* written for the opening of the new Coventry Cathedral in 1962. The text consists of the Latin Requiem Mass, interspersed with war poems by Wilfred Owen, who was killed in the First World War. It was written for three solo singers, a boys' choir, a mixed chorus, a full orchestra and a chamber orchestra. Britten's original idea was that the three soloists should each represent one of the countries that took part in the Second World War – one Russian, one German and one English. The recording of the work was in fact made by the three soloists whom Britten had in mind: Galina Vishnevskaya, wife of the cellist Msistslav Rostropovitch, Peter Pears and Dietrich Fischer-Dieskau. However, at the first performance in Coventry Cathedral on 30 May 1962, Vishnevskaya was unable to appear, so the soprano role was sung by Heather Harper. At the head of the score Britten put a quotation from the preface that Owen had intended to be printed in his collected poems: 'My subject is war, and the pity of war. The poetry is in the pity ... All a poet can do today is warn.'

Britten responded to the challenge of this textural scheme with music of great dramatic and lyrical power, using the old interval of the tritone, both as a structural element within the work, and to achieve contrast.

Britten's next works were commissions. The setting of *Psalm 150* for the centenary of the foundation of his old prep school has instrumentation which can be varied at will according to the availability of the instrumentalists. The composer says simply that it is essential to have a treble instrument, some sort of drum and a keyboard instrument; this is typical of his practical approach to music for amateurs. In the same year (1962) Britten also wrote a *Cantata Misericordium* for the centenary of the International Red Cross, first performed in Geneva in September 1963, and was working on a *Cello Symphony* for Rostropovitch. In 1960 Rostropovitch had asked Britten to write a sonata for him, which they performed together at the Aldeburgh Festival of 1961; Britten then decided to write his *Cello Symphony,* one of the largest of his orchestral works. It was first performed by Rostropovitch in Moscow, and since then has been performed all over the world with Rostropovitch as soloist and Britten as conductor. In 1965 Britten and Pears visited Russia, and Britten set some Pushkin poems in Russian for Vishnevskaya to sing; this song cycle is called *The Poet's Echo,* and was first performed in Moscow in early October 1965.

Britten's fiftieth birthday in 1963 was a landmark in his career, for it showed him starting in a new direction. In the winter of 1955–6 Britten and Pears had visited the Far East on a concert tour, and Britten was greatly impressed by a Japanese Noh play which became the basis of the church opera *Curlew River,* first performed at the 1964 Aldeburgh Festival. It tells the story of a demented mother who, seeking her lost son, finally discovers his grave by the side of the Curlew River. This is the first of Britten's three church operas, which are based on a highly original plan: they are performed by mediæval monks who enter the church in procession at the beginning of the performance, and leave in the same way at the end. The action is highly stylized, all the parts being taken by male voices; for example in *Curlew River* the part of the madwoman is sung by a tenor. The instrumental ensemble is small and mobile, entering the church in procession along with the monks; there is no conductor, and the music follows the principle of heterophony, in which each instrument has its own free rhythm; the players have to keep together by listening to each other. This is a principle which Britten derived from oriental music. The libretti for all three operas were written by William Plomer, who had collaborated with Britten in *Gloriana.* The other two operas are *The Burning Fiery Furnace*, based on the Old Testament story, and *The Prodigal Son*, based on the New Testament story, and all three operas follow the same pattern regarding singers and instrumental ensemble. In these works Britten has aimed at a more austere and less immediately popular style, but nevertheless they have been performed with great success in many other countries besides England. They obviously have a practical advantage in that they do not need elaborate stage settings, and can be performed in any fair-sized church.

Britten's first opera to be specially written for television, *Owen Wingrave*, was first shown in May 1971. Though it uses some television devices such as cross-cutting between different people and different scenes, it consists basically of a number of self-contained episodes with interludes and is quite capable of being presented on stage; in fact Covent Garden have already stated their intention of staging it. The libretto, based on a Henry James story about a young man of military family who refused to join the army, has resemblances to *Billy Budd* in its 'humanitarian' aspects and to *The Turn of the Screw* in its introduction of the supernatural. Musically, Britten does not show anything specifically new in it, but the handling of the medium is effective.

Britten has said that he does not aim to write for posterity, the duration of which may be questionable, but rather for the present. He is interested in writing music which can be performed by non-professionals, and finds it worrying that young composers are not able to write work for young amateurs to play and sing. He usually writes only when he is at home in Aldeburgh. He is still depressed by what he considers to be the basic philistinism of England. He likes to tell how, when leaving school, he was asked what he intended to be, and replied that he wanted to be a composer.

People at the tennis party where this question was asked were amazed and said: 'Yes, but what else?'.

In 1953 Britten was made a Companion of Honour, and in 1965 he was awarded the Order of Merit.

6 British composers since 1940

It is perhaps more than chance that many British composers turned their attention to writing music for films during the War, as there were relatively few performances of new works. Walter Goehr, a former pupil of Schoenberg, put on some concerts of new and unfamiliar works. Edward Clark, secretary of the ISCM's British section, was also able to give some concerts of contemporary music during the war. After the War, despite the fact that the BBC Third Programme was inaugurated in 1946, even modern classics were rarely heard. Stravinsky was usually represented only by his first three ballets; Bartók was seldom played, and Schoenberg, Berg, Webern, the so-called second Viennese school, were hardly heard at all, either on radio or in concert halls.

Soon after the War the Cheltenham Festival of British Contemporary Music was founded; its programmes included a number of new British works, but the programmes tended to be conservative and an over-abundance of well-known classical pieces prevailed. There were, however, some composers whose music was original and worth performing.

One such composer was Alan Bush. Born in London in 1900, he studied at the Royal Academy of Music and in Berlin, and was made Professor of Harmony and Composition at the Royal Academy in 1925. Alan Bush has a very logical mind and it is this quality which characterizes the work which first made him well known, *Dialectic* for string quartet (1929). It is an appropriate title, for the material is argued with contrapuntal mastery and the musical thought is highly concentrated. The use of themes is economical, in keeping with Bush's craftsmanlike compositional theory, which requires that all the melodic material in a work be 'thematic', that is to say, derived from a basic theme. Although in principle this is similar to the twelve-note method, Bush has in fact never been interested in Schoenberg's theory or practice; his music has always remained entirely diatonic. A long-standing member of the Communist Party, he is one of the few English composers to write 'people's music'.

During and after the war Bush produced some notable works, such as the *Lyric Interlude* for violin and piano of 1944, *The Winter Journey,* a very individual Christmas cantata written in 1946, and *Violin Concerto* in 1947, in which the contrast between the soloist and the orchestra is intended to symbolize that of the individual and society.

Bush has also produced several operas. The first of these, *Wat Tyler,* won an Arts Council award in 1951. Although it has been broadcast in England, its first stage production took place in East Germany, where it was a great success. The same applies to *Men of Blackmoor*, written in 1955 and also first produced in East Germany. Extremely effective theatrically because of a fairly simple and direct style, these operas skilfully catch the mood of their historical period. Bush can write simple diatonic music which is at the same time highly original. His latest opera, *Joe Hill* (1970), also produced in East Germany, is based on the life of the American freedom fighter.

Another composer who has worked very much on her own is Priaulx Rainier, the eldest of several women composers who are active in this country. Priaulx Rainier was born in 1903 at Howick, Natal, South Africa, of English-Huguenot parents. She spent her early childhood in a remote part of the country near Zululand, where the music and the language of the natives and the sounds of birds and animals left a lasting impression on her. As a violinist, she earned a scholarship to the Royal Academy in London, which became her permanent home. Because she played the violin professionally for some time after her studies had been completed, she could not turn to composition until she was well over thirty. Her name became known as a composer with the performance of her *Three Greek Epigrams* of 1936 and her *String Quartet* of 1939, which was played in England and abroad. It was not until after the war that she became really well known for her individual, rather chromatic and angular style, which is influenced to some extent by the native music and sounds of South Africa; a good example of this is her *Suite for Clarinet* (1943).

Not all her pieces are based on tribal motifs, however; one of her most successful works was a *Concerto for Cello and Orchestra,* commissioned by the BBC. Another work commissioned by the BBC is *Aequora Lunae* for orchestra, a poetic description of the seas of the moon first performed at Cheltenham in 1967. Priaulx Rainier's works are few: they number about twenty written over a span of more than thirty years, but all show originality and distinction. Though she has never embraced serial technique as such, her works have been tending in the direction of atonality for some time and her style is highly chromatic; her music is strong and passionate and is clearly deeply felt.

Another woman composer of the same generation is Elizabeth Maconchy, born in 1907 of Irish family. She studied with Vaughan Williams at the Royal College of Music and then won a travelling scholarship which took her to Vienna, Paris and Prague; she made a brilliant debut with a piano concerto in 1930, and represented Britain at several pre-war ISCM festivals. She is perhaps best known for her series of string quartets, which show strength as well as imagination and delicacy of writing. She has written a number of instrumental works and also chamber operas, including a comedy, *The Sofa*. Her music has shown some influence of Bartók in tending to revolve around note-centres while making free use of all the notes of the chromatic scale; but she has never used serial technique.

One composer typical of the post-war generation is Peter Racine Fricker. Fricker was born in 1920 and studied at the Royal College of Music. He first became known with his *Four Fughettas* for two pianos (1946) and his *Wind Quintet* (1947). In his music, which is mainly instrumental, he has evolved a remarkably individual idiom which has remained fairly constant throughout his career, recent tendencies toward greater experimentation notwithstanding. Although his writing is chromatic, it never loses the feeling of tonality; some of its semitonal formations are similar to Bartók's but his music resembles neither Bartók or Hindemith, nor that of any other contemporary composer. Despite an occasional flirtation with twelve-tone writing he has never strictly adopted Schoenberg's method. His style makes some use of serial technique, but in Fricker's own individual way: he takes what he needs from it but is not bound by it. His music is predominantly chromatic, but can on occasion contain tonal or even modal elements. His interest in formal exploration and motivic logic sometimes belies the deeply emotional quality of his music and tends to give it an austere appearance.

The *String Quartet No. 1* of 1949, like Schoenberg's first quartet in D minor, compresses all four movements into a continuous musical narrative with great logic which at the same time is completely undoctrinaire; Fricker is bound neither by his models nor by academic rules.

In one of his most successful works, the *Symphony No. 1* of 1949, the Allegro shows the influence of eighteenth-century counterpoint, while a lighter touch and a more open texture can be found in the *Tableau and Dance* movement.

The second string quartet (1953) shows Fricker's contrapuntal skill at its best, while the *Dance Scene* of 1954, more approachable and less austere in style, has remained one of Fricker's most popular works.

After the war Fricker took an active part in teaching at Morley College and in 1952 became its musical director. He retained this position until 1964, when he was invited to go to the University of Santa Barbara, California, as composer in residence. Ultimately he was asked to become permanent head of the music department there. His first work to use twelve-note methods of construction was the *Litany* for double string orchestra of 1955, which contains a twelve-note melody and certain twelve-note harmonic formations. But in general the work is thoroughly tonal and its twelve-note elements may be considered an enrichment rather than an alteration of Fricker's own language. As well as a twelve-note row there is a second theme based on plainsong. Initially the twelve-note row forms another theme, which in turn provides harmonic support for the plainsong. After this first section, however, the plainsong occurs only where it arises naturally out of the note-row. Fricker has often produced rows which are not twelve-note rows; sometimes they contain thirteen notes with one note repeated. Harmonies derived from the row are used freely, often with other material superimposed on them. In other works the row never appears in its original form. Later works contain some twelve-note elements or twelve-note rows, but they appear merely on the surface of the music, as it were. Increasingly, Fricker tends to avoid octave doublings, and although he uses certain ideas derived from Schoenbergian technique, he never commits himself to it strictly.

Fricker's fourth symphony, commissioned by the City of Birmingham Orchestra and performed in 1967, is one of his strongest and most impressive works. His *Nocturne* for chamber orchestra, written for the Cheltenham Festival of 1971, has a brooding atmospheric quality combined with powerful dramatic outbursts.

In speaking of his work, Fricker has said:

> I feel myself as an archaeologist rather than an architect of musical space. For me it's more a process of uncovering something that is already there. To a certain extent I feel I am building something, but, because my work seems to be achieving an independent existence, I feel more as if I am excavating, scraping away different layers to reveal it. If I'm not getting on well I feel it is because I haven't cleared away the debris so that I can see the work clearly.

However Fricker has said that he always conceives a piece as a whole before he starts writing a note. He also believes in starting with a fragment from which the whole of the work can be derived; he says, for instance, that the first bar and a half of his *Rapsodia Concertante* occurred to him by inspiration, 'if you like', and by studying it he found that it could be analysed as a twelve-note idea. From this he derived a row, a chord system and various melodic sequences which occur throughout the entire work. On the question of style, he does not think it unreasonable for a composer to have to repeat himself, and feels that his own style has become 'leaner' in recent years. On occasion he has been inspired by the music of other composers; for instance, the scherzo of his octet was suggested by the *Queen Mab Scherzo* from Berlioz's *Romeo and Juliet.* Fascinated by this particular movement, he wanted to try and recreate it in his own language.

Twelve-note music came rather late to England. The first British composers to use this technique were Elisabeth Lutyens and myself, round about 1939. We were joined by three composers from abroad: Egon Wellesz from Austria, Roberto Gerhard from Spain and Mátyás Seiber from Hungary. But not all these composers were writing twelve-note music all the time, and indeed several wrote a good many tonal works as well as their twelve-note compositions. In general, this kind of music was not well received by the public, most of whom thought that all twelve-note composers were mad. As an example of the kind of attitude which obtained even in later years, I can quote a review of a very early piece of mine, *Night Music,* which is vaguely atonal but is not even a twelve-note piece. When the score was published in 1949, *Musical Opinion* wrote: 'This work is dedicated to Anton Webern on his sixtieth birthday (1943), and as one might expect from such a dedication, is atonal, gaunt in style and melodically spiky. There is nothing in this work to suggest that the composer is British – or doesn't that matter to British composers any more?' This chauvinistic attitude derives of course from the domination of Vaughan Williams and the folk-song school, to which all British composers were expected (by some people) to adhere.

Elisabeth Lutyens was born in London on 9 July 1906, the third daughter of the architect Sir Edwin Lutyens. Her family was not musical, but did not actively oppose her interest in music. Fortunately, having a private income, she was able to choose her own profession. By the time she was nine or ten she had started writing little pieces and when she was sixteen she went to Paris to study solfège and piano at the École Normale. After living for two years in India and Australia she spent four years at the Royal College of Music. In 1931 she returned to Paris to study with Georges Caussade. Two years later her ballet, *The Birthday of the Infanta,* after Oscar Wilde, was produced by the Camargo Society in London. Between 1936 and 1939 she wrote a good deal of chamber music. Her *String Trio,* written in 1939, has a passionate style which apparently derives as much from the second Viennese school as from Bartók, but in fact at this time she had never seen any scores of Schoenberg or Webern.

Her first twelve-note work was the *Concerto* for nine instruments, finished in 1941, the year in which she married Edward Clark. In the *Concerto* she discovered the principles of serial music for herself. Later, scores of the second Viennese school did become available, which saved her from wasting time. Lutyens is unhappy now about some of her earlier works, though at that time they created a considerable impression.

During the war her *Concerto* for nine instruments was

performed in America and in London; in 1949 her dramatic scene, *The Pit,* with a text by W. R. Rodgers, was given a stage production at the ISCM festival in Palermo. Another wartime work was the set of five *Intermezzi* for piano (1942). These combine a twelve-note structure with traditional motivic shapes, as do some subsequent works, such as her *Viola Concerto* of 1947 and the *String Quartet No. 3* of 1948, where the twelve-note writing is combined with normal types of rhythm. The last movement of the *Viola Concerto,* as well as the last of the *Three Symphonic Preludes,* is based on a passacaglia form. With the *String Quartet No. 6* of 1952, the rhythms have become very much freer, more ingenious and more complex, and the compression of thought is greater; the slow movement is enclosed by a repeat of the allegro first movement. Lutyens has said that she wrote this quartet at one sitting in something like twelve hours – the first time she has ever worked at such speed. The quartet is dedicated to the painter Francis Bacon; Lutyens has always been interested in the visual arts and has a son who is a painter.

In 1953 Lutyens wrote one of her best known works, the *Motet* Opus 27, a setting of a text by the Austrian philosopher Wittgenstein, which shows a mastery of modern vocal counterpoint. Her *Capricci* for two harps and percussion and *Sonance* for horn and piano show her penchant for unusual and neglected instrumental combinations, while the *Duo for Cello and Piano* illustrates her interest in canonic writing, often with canons in inversion or augmentation.

The first of her vocal works of this period, *O saisons, O châteaux* of 1946, a setting of Rimbaud's poem for soprano, guitar, harp, solo violin and strings, is one of her most sensitive and successful works and was the forerunner of her present mature style. This is highly atmospheric, but at the same time logically constructed: every note is of importance, and there are no 'impressionist' washes of sound. At the same time there is a wide variety of colour; the music is often based on small thematic fragments rather than themes in the old sense.

Despite the fact that Lutyens came late to composition, she has written a considerable number of works. Her opus numbers up to 1967 had reached sixty-seven; though nearly all short, her pieces are extremely concentrated. One of the most interesting and successful pieces of recent years is the *Symphonies* Opus 46, for solo piano, wind, harps and percussion, commissioned by the BBC for the 1962 Proms. It takes the form of a palindrome, with a climax in the middle and both sides parallel. It also calls for an unusual orchestral seating plan. Explaining the necessity of the plan, Lutyens maintained that the standard orchestra is constructed chiefly for the performance of eighteenth- and nineteenth-century music consisting of a tune, middle and bass in triadic harmony, with a complete harmonic chord in each section of the orchestra. In modern music, however, each instrument is a soloist, there are no octave and very few unison doublings, so the orchestra now becomes a large chamber group. Lutyens agrees with Stravinsky that the standard orchestra is out of date and therefore of use only to out of date composers. Most of her recent orchestral works have, in fact, been written for a large chamber group, rather than for a normal orchestra.

Edward Clark died in 1962; in 1966 Elisabeth Lutyens's sixtieth birthday brought tributes in the form of birthday concerts given by the BBC and the Macnaghten Society. Her sixty-fifth birthday in 1971 was celebrated by the BBC with a series of six broadcast concerts of her music from all periods of her career; her 'charade' *Time Off?* was performed in 1972 by the New Opera Company at Sadler's Wells.

Apart from her own work as a composer, Lutyens has always encouraged young composers with her advice. She feels that whereas at most colleges one is merely taught to write a pastiche of one or two composers such as Palestrina, Bach and Brahms, the compositional procedures of all composers throughout musical history should be made available and analysed.

Egon Wellesz was born in Vienna on 21 October 1885. He attended the University of Vienna, where he studied harmony with Karl Frühling and the history of music with Guido Adler. He found Adler an excellent teacher and his lectures most stimulating. Adler was a friend of Mahler's and obtained permission for his own and Schoenberg's pupils to attend Mahler's rehearsals; thus Wellesz not only heard Mahler conduct the first performances of his own symphonies, but also heard him make corrections before these performances. According to Wellesz, Mahler was in the habit of altering details in the orchestration of his works to suit the acoustics of the hall in which they were being performed, and so introduced the concept of the relative into orchestration.

From 1904 to 1906 Wellesz studied counterpoint, fugue and composition with Schoenberg, at the same time as Berg and Webern. Wellesz regarded Schoenberg as a great composition teacher; he believed in the workshop method of the Old Masters, keeping in close contact with his pupils. When he criticised their work he always gave four or five different solutions to the problems they were trying to solve, believing that every artistic problem was capable of a variety of solutions. He insisted however that one must always strive for integrity of thought, never, for example, harmonizing a simple melody in a complicated way to make it sound more 'interesting'. When he liked a piece he was shown he would often make suggestions for slight modifications, taking an interest even in minute details. He felt strongly that none of his pupils should have their works published until they were technically mature, and Wellesz was twenty-five before his first composition was published. This was a set of piano pieces which had been performed in Budapest, where Béla Bartók had heard them and liked them so much that he took them to his own publisher.

From 1906 onwards Wellesz worked on his own as a

composer, having been advised by Bruno Walter that his music was based more on Viennese classical tradition than on Schoenberg's methods. Schoenberg has always had a certain influence on Wellesz's music, however.

Wellesz took his Doctor of Philosophy degree at Vienna in 1908 with a thesis on Giuseppe Benno, a composer of Italian origin who lived in Vienna in the middle of the eighteenth century. He was forced to decide whether to become a scholar or a conductor, as there was no opportunity for a young composer to earn a living in the Vienna of that time. Even for a conductor opportunities were limited, as there were only a few concerts during the season; when Mahler performed his own symphonies, for instance, he paid the orchestra out of his own pocket. Rather than become conductor of a provincial orchestra, Wellesz chose an academic career because it would give him more free time for composing. The only other alternative would have been to orchestrate operettas like Schoenberg, who was able to earn money only by scoring thousands of pages.

In 1913 Wellesz was appointed a lecturer in musical history at the University of Vienna. He continued his researches into baroque opera, but also became interested in a new subject, Byzantine music. Wanting to investigate the sources of Western music, and to discover whether it really started with Gregorian chant or went back to a more ancient tradition, he spent several years studying the history of the liturgy in the Eastern churches, trying to find the secrets of that kind of homophonic music; at that time Byzantine musical notation had not yet been deciphered. Wellesz suddenly found the solution by asking himself: why are so many signs used in such an odd way? He realized that it was an economical system which combined interval signs with signs of execution. This discovery led to the complete deciphering of Byzantine notation, which had previously been impossible. It meant that not only the notes, but also the rhythms could be deciphered, and Wellesz feels that these rhythms can now be reproduced even more accurately than those of Gregorian chant. Moreover, Wellesz found that Byzantine music was constructed from a number of formulae over which the composer improvised. That is, the composer would start with a simple line which, over the course of centuries, had often been embellished in a very complicated manner. Wellesz felt that Eastern music was based on a principle of construction similar to that discovered by Schoenberg when he developed his serial methods.

Wellesz's earlier works were mainly chamber music and were influenced by Mahler and Debussy, as well as by Schoenberg. They show great concentration and an advanced tonality and were, of course, written at a time when nobody but Schoenberg and a few of his followers were writing atonal music. During the First World War, Wellesz met the other composer who had begun to use a twelve-note system, Josef Matthias Hauer, and introduced him to Schoenberg. They naturally became extremely interested in each other's methods, though they went their different ways. According to Wellesz, Hauer was slightly crazy. He wanted to write music 'like the ancient Greeks', and had, in fact discovered a system of twelve-note composition which he called Nomos. Unlike Schoenberg, who worked out his rows most carefully, Hauer put his together quite haphazardly, even handing people cards and asking them to put them in any order they liked. Nevertheless, some of his pieces are beautiful and have been fairly successful.

Wellesz really wanted to be a dramatic composer, and between 1918 and 1930 he wrote five operas and four ballets, which were successfully produced in Austria and Germany. Some of these are based on classical subjects; Wellesz has said that he was interested in Greek tragedy, and his aim was to continue the line of the great Austrian tradition. However, this meant that he could not continue writing in the minute, concentrated style of Schoenberg or that of his own early chamber works. His first opera, *Princess Girnara*, was based on a Buddhist legend, with a libretto by

Jacob Wasserman. Next Wellesz wrote a ballet, *Achilles on Skyros,* with a libretto by Hofmannsthal (though this was not disclosed at the time, as Hofmannsthal was writing libretti for Strauss and did not want to be discovered collaborating with another composer).

Wellesz also wrote an opera, *Alkestis,* again with a text by Hofmannsthal: produced in 1924, this was one of the great successes of its day. It created a new kind of operatic form, using a chorus, dance pantomime and coloratura arias as the pivots of the musical design. In a sense, Wellesz was returning to the ideas of Gluck and the baroque opera, a style he had studied and knew well. The music could be described as diatonic in a way, but it is largely polytonal, so that there is hardly a common chord in the whole opera. Then followed an opera based on an Aztec legend, *The Sacrifice of the Prisoner,* first performed in 1926; this, together with *Achilles on Skyros* and *Alkestis,* forms a kind of trilogy. In 1928 came an opera on Goethe's *Scherz, List und Rache,* and finally, *The Bacchae* (1931). All these operas, and other stage works, though showing the influence of Schoenberg, are in the main diatonic, making use of motoric rhythms, and base their structural principles on the baroque opera and cantata.

Meanwhile Wellesz was continuing with his academic work and in 1924 published the first book to appear on Schoenberg. In 1932 he was given an honorary doctorate at Oxford, to celebrate the bicentenary of the birth of Haydn; the university felt that of all Viennese musicians, Wellesz was the most fitting recipient. In 1925 Wellesz formulated his own attitude to dramatic music:

> I have in mind the idea of a dramatic work of art in which song shall collaborate with the dance in artistic expression. Such a form can only be realised from materials which are at once timeless and bounded by time, and through which is afforded a vision of a higher world.

This religious and spiritual feeling characterizes the works Wellesz wrote in the 1930s. They show an increasing clarity in harmonic and tonal methods and a growing ease of rhythmic movement. They tend towards a polyphonic texture which recalls the motet types of the sixteenth century, and include the sacred cantata *Mitte des Lebens,* some works for male chorus and two masses, in F minor and C major.

In 1938 Wellesz was invited to visit England, where he lectured on opera in London and Cambridge. While he was in England the *Anschluss* took place, and he was unable to return to Vienna because of his Jewish origins. He has remained in England ever since. For a time he concentrated on his academic work, but in 1943 began to compose again, stimulated by English seventeenth-century and medieval poetry.

Between 1944 and 1948 he wrote three more string quartets to add to the four he had written earlier, and also two symphonies, in C and E flat. His music at this period was very much more diatonic than it had been in the past; this can be seen in his cantata to words by Gerard Manley Hopkins, *The Leaden Echo and the Golden Echo.* In the same year he published another book, *Eastern Elements in Western Chant,* and in the following year *The History of Byzantine Music and Hymnography.* His recent string quartets and his fifth and sixth symphonies show a renewal of interest in atonal and twelve-tone music. His *Symphony No. 5* begins with a row of seven notes which is extended to twelve in the course of the first movement; although each movement has its own row, all four movements are held together by a recurring group of four notes. Wellesz believes that whatever happens there must always be a line of continuity connecting us to the great heritage of western civilization, including the writing of music, which can be memorized and retained in the mind. His seventh symphony, though based on serial technique, is subtitled *Against the Stream* because of its adherence to this belief. At the time of writing Wellesz, at eighty-six, is still active both as composer and scholar and in spite of his links with the past, his mind is very much looking towards the future.

Roberto Gerhard was born at Valls near Tarragona on 25 September 1896. His father wanted him to enter the family business, and he was sent to study at the *École de Commerce* at Neuchâtel in Switzerland. However, Gerhard decided even at this stage to devote himself to music, and he was able to overcome parental opposition. In 1915 he went to study the piano with Granados, and after Granados's tragic death studied with Pedrell, the founder of modern Spanish music. Pedrell was a much greater teacher than composer; his endless researches span the gulf between the Spanish polyphonic and lutenist tradition and the great heritage of folk music. From him Gerhard absorbed the music of the classical Spanish polyphonic age, and while studying with him published two works. The first was a setting of poems by Lopez Pico in which a lyrical vocal line is supported by a piano accompaniment; this was freer and more imaginative than anything his master had written.

Next came his *Piano Trio* (1918), which was strongly influenced by French impressionism, though it has a rhythmical interest which goes far beyond similar works of the French school.

After studying with Pedrell for five years, Gerhard realized that he could learn no more from him; he therefore left him in 1921 and spent the next two years studying the craft of composition on his own. During this period he discovered *Pierrot Lunaire,* understanding both its intellectual importance and its colouristic aspect. Under the influence of *Pierrot,* Gerhard produced two aphoristic sketches for piano and a set of seven Japanese poems for voice and chamber ensemble.

About this time Gerhard read an article by Wellesz mentioning Schoenberg's capabilities as a teacher. After an exchange of letters, Gerhard left Spain for Vienna and in 1923 joined Schoenberg's composition class. He studied with Schoenberg in Berlin as well as in Vienna for the next five years, confining his activities to the exercises and studies that were set him. On leaving Schoenberg in 1928, however, he wrote a full-scale work as a kind of testament to what he had learnt, the *Quintet for Wind Instruments.* This work is the first example of the ingenious way in which Gerhard fuses national and cosmopolitan elements. In it he breaks away from the traditionally Parisian affinities of Spanish composers, and also avoids following Schoenberg's system blindly; instead, he uses the pattern in his own way, treating the note-series in sections and making interpolations and repetitions, so that he is able to avoid applying the system mechanically. The music is thought out note by note rather than computed mathematically. He avoids the tortuous melodic lines often found in the Viennese School and erects his subtle contrapuntal structure on a firm base, over a framework of vivacious rhythms. 'In the last of his four movements it would not be fanciful to detect the sound of laughter,' writes David Drew.

After returning to Spain, Gerhard held a position as professor at the Barcelona *Escola Normal de la Generalitat.* In 1932 he also became head of the music department of the Catalan Library, and from 1937–8 was on the Central Music Council of the Spanish Republican government. After the defeat of the Republican government in the civil war, Gerhard and his Austrian wife left Spain and went to Cambridge, where he was given a research fellowship at King's College. Since then and till his death in 1970, he lived in Cambridge, both composing and giving private lessons.

Gerhard's *Albada, Interludi y Dança* was performed at the London ISCM Festival of 1938. This last piece was written in 1937 for the BBC's series of programmes of Spanish music. A note on the work for the ISCM performance says: 'The composer's circumstances were those of Spain today, dominated by one element – the tension of popular feeling'. *Albada* or *Aubade* was the name given by the troubadours of Provence and Catalonia to a form of song designed to greet the dawn. In Catalonia this name is still given to music played by little bands of wind instruments which parade through the village streets in the early morning on festival days. Thus the *Albada* is the antithesis of a nocturne, and here Gerhard writes a kind of morning serenade with tunes which are popular in spirit, though not in origin.

In 1942 Gerhard began work on a second violin concerto (he left the first unfinished). It was performed at the Florence *Maggio* in 1950. This is a remarkable work, with a great deal of Spanish feeling, in which twelve-note and tonal writing meet. It again illustrates his original and exciting command of the orchestra, and has a classical strength which saves it from the excesses of the later romantic school. In the last movement Gerhard was even able to make allusions to Sarasate without making the music sound incongruous.

In the fifties, Gerhard began to take up a new attitude towards twelve-note technique, derived from a study of the later works of Schoenberg. He elaborated this new principle in an article in *The Score* of May 1952, saying: 'Though all twelve notes are equal, some are more equal than others'. In his piano concerto of 1950, although it is a twelve-note work, the note C does predominate. Gerhard also noted the importance of permutation in twelve-note music, the rearrangement of notes within the component chords. In the works of this period he was close to Schoenberg but as usual was writing in his individual way.

The *Symphony No. 1* of 1953 starts a new period in Gerhard's development. Though the thematic material tends to become more and more concise and even to disappear altogether, the composer uses all available contemporary resources in constructing large-scale forms in his own way, and does this without any loss of spontaneity. Gerhard also made many experiments in *musique concrète* and electronic music; in fact some of his later orchestral works sound like electronic music without using electronic machines. Gerhard was able to use these sounds in an architectural way, not merely for a pointillist or colouristic effect. This is partly evident in the *String Quartet* of 1955 and particularly in the *Symphony No. 2* of 1959. The latter work creates the effect of a symphony without any immediately recognizable thematic material.

Gerhard's music was unjustly neglected for far too long; apart from occasional and rather sporadic performances, he was not heard for many years. But in the last ten years his music has come more and more into its own. He received a number of commissions, especially during Sir William Glock's term as head of music at the BBC.

Gerhard's *Hymnody* for three wind instruments, four brass, percussion and two pianos was written in 1962–3 and first performed on 23 May 1963 at a BBC invitation concert by the Virtuoso Ensemble. The critics not only praised Gerhard's technique but noted the sensuous gratification and inventive vitality of the music. Another work, *Collages* for tape recorder and orchestra, actually combines electronic sounds with orchestral ones. A larger work was *The Plague,* based on Albert Camus's text in a translation by Stuart Gilbert; this is a cantata for speaker, chorus and orchestra, lasting about forty-five minutes. It was first performed on 1 April 1964 in London by the BBC. The critics were again impressed by 'its bursts of musical imagination and the sustained humanistic high-mindedness of its conception'. Probably the most remarkable of his later works is the *Concerto for Orchestra,* first performed by the BBC orchestra on 25 April 1965 in Boston, during their tour of America. This most impressive score is full of extraordinary sounds; it was described as 'a strange and fascinating world of as yet uncharted possibilities, and a brilliant essay in orchestral technique'. Gerhard uses a whole range of unusual effects, and yet manages to give the work an architectural shape.

Between then and the end of his life in 1970 Gerhard wrote several further important works, including three of a projected series of twelve chamber works based on the signs of the zodiac. Gerhard discussed his interpretation of serial technique in his contribution to Josef Rufer's first edition of *Composition with Twelve Notes.* In Schoenberg's later works the development rather than being linear is spiral or circular, turning, he says, in complete revolutions around the centre, from which all the possibilities provided by the basic idea are systematically explored. This gives rise to a 'polarity' which counteracts the principle of the unalterability of the order of the notes within the series by the principle of permutation mentioned above. Thus as early as bars three to eight of the opera *Von Heute auf Morgen* Schoenberg uses both halves of the series in permutations which are, in fact, identical with the scale-like arrangement of the hexachords on which the series is based. Gerhard considers this treatment to be legitimate because it rests on Rameau's principle that the different inversions of the triad are harmonically identical, being different aspects of the same concept of sound. By extension this implies that the twelve notes of a series need not always appear in the same order, since the order of the notes comprising a chord within the series can be altered in many different ways. This is corroborated by Schoenberg's axiom of the unity of musical space, in which the horizontal and vertical are treated as different aspects, though identical in substance, of the one musical 'object'. Speaking of the intelligibility of modern music, Gerhard quoted T. S. Eliot's remark on the 'meaning' of a poem, which serves 'to satisfy one habit of the reader, to keep his mind diverted and quiet, while the poem does its work upon him; much as the imaginary burglar is always provided with a bit of nice meat for the house-dog'. Gerhard felt that a serial technique fulfils a comparable function in the creative process of a composer.

Mátyás Seiber was born in Budapest on 4 May 1905. His mother taught the piano and her children all joined together in chamber music; his brother and sister both became professional musicians. Seiber learnt to play the cello from the age of ten, and studied music at a secondary school up to the age of eighteen.

When he was only fourteen he also took lessons in composition at the Budapest Academy with Kodály. His early works, written while he was still a student, show three influences: Gregorian chant, in the *Missa Brevis* for unaccompanied choir of 1924; folk music, in his arrangement of *Three Hungarian Folksongs* for piano of 1922; and that of Kodály, in his first string quartet of 1924.

In 1925 Seiber went to Frankfurt, where he taught at a private music school; then, longing for adventure, he joined a ship's orchestra and visited North, Central and South America. Unfortunately the food on the ship was so bad that it gave him stomach trouble which lasted the rest of his life.

In 1925 Seiber had written a *Wind Sextet* which was thought by the jury to be the best work at a competition in Budapest, but it was not given the prize; Bartók, who was one of the judges, resigned from the jury in protest. In 1928 Seiber joined Hoch's Conservatoire in Frankfurt, as director of the newly formed jazz department; this appointment caused a considerable upheaval among the older and more conservative teachers. Seiber also conducted at the *Neues Theater*, the *Schauspielhaus* and some local choral societies. In addition, he became the cellist of the Lenzewski Quartet, gave cello recitals in Germany and wrote reviews for a Hungarian paper. Works of this period include a *Sonata da Camera* for violin and cello of 1925, a *Divertimento* for clarinet and string quartet of 1926, some *Rhythmic Studies* for piano of 1933, and *Four Hungarian Folksongs* for two violins of 1932. Several works reflect the atmosphere of the Weimar Republic, such as *Two Jazzolettes,* which were experiments in jazz chamber music (1929 and 1932), and settings of *Three Nonsense Songs* by Christian Morgenstern for soprano and clarinet. In 1933 Seiber visited Budapest, Moscow and Leningrad as music correspondent, and two years later he settled in England, where he remained to the end of his life, and where his first job was as an adviser to a firm of music publishers.

So far Seiber's works had been influenced mainly by Hungarian models, and to some extent by neo-classicism in the *Clarinet Quintet* and the *Sonata da Camera,* but in 1934–5, shortly before coming to England, he wrote a second string quartet which was a twelve-note work, although he was fairly free in his handling of the series. In the main theme of the first movement, for example, the first violin plays the first eight notes with several repetitions of the first group of four notes; during these repetitions the remaining four notes are divided into various symmetrical groups so that all twelve notes are present but not in the order of the series. Seiber did not use the twelve-note method consistently until towards the end of his life.

In 1942 he joined the staff of Morley College, teaching music appreciation and composition as well as conducting the orchestra. Probably the most important of Seiber's war-time works is the *Fantasia Concertante* for violin and string orchestra of 1943–4. This was first performed under the German composer and conductor Walter Goehr in London in 1945, and was also given at the Palermo ISCM festival of 1949. It is again based on a twelve-note series fairly freely handled. Sometimes the tonal material is divided into four triads and there are sections where the violin plays completely free passages against a twelve-note orchestral accompaniment.

Seiber's finest creative period came during the years after the Second World War. It began with the cantata *Ulysses,* written in 1946–7. This is a setting of the passage from Joyce's *Ulysses* where Bloom takes Stephen out into his garden and shows him 'the heaventree of stars hung with humid nightblue fruit'. It is a most sensitive and poetical work. Its third movement uses a symmetrical tone-row made up alternately of minor thirds and minor seconds; the second half is an inversion of the first, but the fugue theme which is formed from it is handled quite freely, so in fact only the principle of the minor thirds separated by minor seconds survives. The fourth movement of *Ulysses,* which is called *Nocturne,* is based on a quotation from Schoenberg, the two chords from his *Piano Piece Opus 19 No. 6.* Seiber added two complementary chords to the original two, so that the complete four make up all the twelve notes of the scale. The whole movement is built on these four chords and on the melodic lines derived from them, but the composer has taken liberties, as for instance in a passage where the solo voice winds freely round the chords, which are confined to the orchestra. Seiber commented on his approach to twelve-note writing in these words: 'I suppose that orthodox twelve-note composers and theoreticians will say that this is not proper twelve-note writing. That seems to me of not the least importance at the moment; the only thing that interests me is whether I succeeded in writing some real *music*'.

Seiber's next important work was the third quartet subtitled *Quartetto Lirico,* written between 1948 and 1951. As its title implies, it is a somewhat romantic and lyrical work; it has affinities with Berg's *Lyric Suite.* Throughout his life Seiber was a prolific composer of incidental music for radio, plays and films, the most important of these being the music for both parts of Goethe's *Faust,* written in 1949 in collaboration with Louis MacNeice for the BBC; and music for the George Orwell film, *Animal Farm.* In 1953 came the song cycle *To Poetry* for tenor and piano, and also the *Elegy* for viola and small orchestra. Although not a twelve-note work, its opening bars contain all the material for the whole piece, and the second subject is in fact a twelve-note theme, though it has no significance as such in the rest of the work. The work is in ternary form with leanings towards sonata form. The *Concert Piece* for violin and piano of 1954 is characterized by a very individual and strict permutatory use of a basic series, and is one of Seiber's most experimental works. In 1956 came the *Tre Pezzi* for cello and orchestra, and in the following year Seiber returned to Joyce for his chamber cantata, *Three Fragments from A Portrait of the Artist as a Young Man,* written for speaker, chorus and instrumental ensemble. It is a strictly twelve-note work and it is dedicated to the memory of a friend of Seiber's, the composer Erich Kahn. Though sparser in texture than any of his earlier works, it still retains the poetry of *Ulysses.*

In 1958 Seiber wrote the *Permutazione a Cinque* for wind quintet, one of the few works of his to make use of the permutation system. His last work was the ballet *The Invitation,* written for Covent Garden, with choreography by Kenneth Macmillan. The theme of the ballet is the seduction of innocence, and it was first performed at Oxford in November 1960, coming to Covent Garden the following month. But by this time Seiber had already died a tragic death. While in South Africa during the summer of 1960, he was travelling in a car in the Kruger National Park when the steering wheel came off and the car hit a tree. Seiber was killed instantly. He will be remembered as a composer of great imagination and enormous craftsmanship and as a teacher of genius.

I am very hesitant to write about myself, and should make it clear that I am doing so only at the request of the publisher. I was born in Oxford on 26 August 1915; my paternal grandfather's family were musicians in Devonshire, and he himself trained as an organist. My mother's father, Sir William Schlich, came from Darmstadt in Germany; though my mother was born in England, she has in fact no English blood. My parents were in Burma when I was young; they were not particularly musical, but I was allowed to have piano lessons at school. However I did not really become interested in music until I went to Winchester at the age of thirteen. Here I met two boys who later became well known in the musical world, Robert Irving, now musical director of the New York City Ballet, and James Robertson, now director of the London Opera Centre. A gramophone in our rooms at school helped us to get to know not only all the classical repertoire, but a number of works which were then considered modern, such as Stravinsky's *Rite of Spring* and Honegger's *Pacific 231* and *Rugby*.

I now began to try to compose; our music master, Dr George Dyson, later director of the Royal College of Music, started giving me harmony lessons, and by the time I left school I had got far enough to have a short composition played by the school orchestra. I now wanted to take up music as a professional career, but I had won a classical scholarship to Oxford, and therefore had to continue studying classics and philosophy for another four years. However in my spare time at Oxford I was given some harmony lessons by Dr Sydney Watson, the organist of New College. My chief revelation while at Oxford was the first English performance of *Wozzeck*, given by the BBC under Sir Adrian Boult, which knocked me absolutely sideways. I determined to try and find out more about this kind of music. About that time Dr Theodor Wiesengrund-Adorno, a former pupil of Schoenberg and Webern, came to Oxford as a refugee from Nazi Germany.

Later Sir Hugh Allen, who was professor of music at Oxford as well as director of the Royal College, promised me a travelling scholarship after I took my degree at Oxford. I did this in 1937 and then went to the College in spite of the opposition of my parents, who wanted me to sit for the Civil Service exam. I had become a great admirer of the ballet and was passionately interested in Berlioz and Liszt.

While at Oxford I had written a few small pieces and Sir Hugh Allen suggested that I should show these to William Walton. I found him very helpful, and he suggested that while I was at the College I should have lessons with John Ireland. I liked Ireland very much as a person, but studied with him only for a comparatively short time. When I went to the College, my previous allowance from my parents was stopped, and I had to earn my living by teaching logic to a clergyman in Mornington Crescent.

In the autumn of 1937 I went to Vienna to study with Webern; Adorno wrote to him and arranged the lessons. I have described my lessons with Webern in the introduction to Wildgan's biography of him. We went through Schoenberg's *Harmonielehre* very thoroughly from beginning to end and Webern also gave me some analyses of his own works. Apart from my lessons with Webern I went to the Vienna Conservatoire for various general courses, including conducting and musical history. I went to the opera nearly every night. My scholarship money ran out after a few months and so I had to return to England, leaving Vienna just about a fortnight before Hitler's troops arrived.

On returning to England I went back to the College as I felt I did not know enough about counterpoint. I also took lessons in orchestration and conducting. But my studies there were cut short, as it was necessary for me to get a regular job. The BBC were advertising for a chorus librarian; I applied for this job and got it. This meant that I had had only about one year's musical training, apart from a few lessons at school and university. My job at the BBC consisted mostly of carting two hundred and fifty copies of the *Messiah* round London and distributing them to members of the BBC Choral Society. I had not written any music since before going to Webern, as I felt that I needed to change my style radically. I started again early in 1939 and wrote a rather hybrid piece with some elements of Webern and some of Liszt. A friend put up the money for me to give a concert with the London String Orchestra in April 1939 and I performed this piece there, together with Liszt's *Malediction,* works by van Dieren and Thomas Roseingrave and the first public performance in England of Webern's *Five Pieces Opus 5* in the orchestral version. This concert showed me that I was not very experienced either as a composer or as a conductor, but nevertheless I went on writing music in my spare time, and finished two twelve-tone works – a set of piano variations and a string quartet – during 1939.

When the war started the BBC music department moved to Bristol, and I went there in early 1940. During the period

I spent some time at the house of John Davenport at Marshfield, near Bristol. His house party included William Glock, later controller of music at the BBC, the composers Lennox Berkeley and Arnold Cooke, the poets William Empson and Dylan Thomas, together with the latter's wife Caitlin and the critic Henry Boys – highly stimulating company, which I enjoyed very much. I joined the army in March 1940 and after a short period in Bristol with the Gloucestershire Regiment was transferred to the Intelligence Corps and thence to a remote part of the Scottish Highlands. Here I was able to start composing again; I eventually produced a piece which I now call Opus 1, the *Suite for String Orchestra,* which was first performed in London in 1943 by Walter Goehr. At this period I did not feel experienced enough to write strict twelve-note music, so I wrote in a kind of atonal style which was partly influenced by Bartók. Walter Goehr's concert began with Webern's orchestration of the *Ricercare* from Bach's *Musical Offering,* and my next work, *Night Music,* took its orchestral style from Webern's arrangement; I wrote it in honour of Webern's sixtieth birthday in December 1943.

After this I continued to compose whenever I had the opportunity; when I was later transferred to various Special Operations Executive establishments in southern England as an instructor, I could sometimes work in the evenings. At the end of the war I was posted to Germany and spent the winter of 1945–6 at Rhine Army headquarters, mostly concerned with assisting Hugh Trevor-Roper in his investigation into the death of Hitler. At this time I wrote the *Second Nocturne* for chamber orchestra; this was prompted by hearing of the tragic and senseless death of Webern in September 1945.[1]

When I was demobilized in 1946 I went back to the BBC, this time as a producer of musical programmes. The Third Programme was about to start, and it was possible to put on much interesting and enterprising music. I tried to support twelve-note music by putting on the works not only of

Schoenberg, Berg and Webern but of younger composers such as Dallapiccola and Elisabeth Lutyens; in doing so I met a certain amount of opposition from the higher-ups. Meanwhile my *Second Nocturne* had been played as an interlude in the ballet at Sadler's Wells and a performance of this was heard by René Leibowitz, the French composer who was the leader of the twelve-tone school in Paris and taught Boulez. He suggested that I should write a strictly twelve-note piece for his chamber ensemble in Paris, so I composed the *Intermezzo for Eleven Instruments*, which I dedicated to the memory of Webern and which was performed by Leibowitz and his ensemble at a short festival of contemporary music in Paris early in 1947. I followed this with a number of short twelve-note works, but did not yet feel able to attempt a big one. However the opportunity came shortly afterwards. Edith Sitwell sent me a copy of her *Gold Coast Customs*, which I had never read, and which impressed me tremendously. I decided to make it into a work for speakers, male chorus and a rather peculiar orchestra which included wind, brass, two pianos and a good deal of percussion but no upper strings.

I was very occupied by the BBC and could compose only in the evenings or at weekends. In 1947 Edward Dent retired from the presidency of the ISCM and Edward Clark was elected in his place; he asked me if I would take over his old job as general secretary of the ISCM. I did this for some time, on a spare-time and voluntary basis, but in 1948 it was decided that the general secretaryship should be a full-time paid job. Wanting to have more time to compose, I resigned from the BBC in October 1948. Unfortunately, however, the funds provided by the foreign sections which financed the ISCM were not large enough to pay for a full-time general secretary, so I was eventually compelled to resign from the post in 1949. Meanwhile I had settled in St John's Wood; there I met my first wife, Lesley Gray.

From this time onwards I worked freelance, living by teaching, lecturing and occasionally writing books; for a long time I found it difficult to get commissions for incidental music, being feared as a twelve-tone composer. *Gold Coast Customs* was performed in May 1949 with Edith Sitwell and Constant Lambert reciting, and was repeated twice by the BBC in the same year. My next work was the *Poem for Twenty-Two Strings,* written as a wedding present for my wife and performed in 1950 at the Darmstadt Summer School by Hermann Scherchen.

Scherchen took an interest in me from then onwards and gave the first performance of my next work, *The Riverrun,* a setting for speaker and orchestra of part of the final passage of Joyce's *Finnegans Wake.* This was first performed in Düsseldorf in 1951 and Scherchen gave the first English performances in Liverpool and London in 1955. I completed the trilogy of works for speakers and orchestra with *The Shadow of Cain* (1952); this was first performed at the Palace Theatre, London, with Edith Sitwell and Dylan Thomas, and later Dylan Thomas recited the whole speaking part himself, this time at the Winter Proms. Scherchen now asked me to write an orchestral work for him, and I produced my first symphony. I was a little worried about writing a twelve-note symphony, as there were not many examples of such a thing at this time, and I used mainly classical forms, though the intermezzo between the slow movement and finale is a kind of free fugato. Scherchen conducted its première in Hamburg in 1954. In the middle fifties I tried to write one or two works in a free atonal style without any definite series – but I did not feel very happy with this style, and returned to the twelve-note technique in all my work from 1957 onwards. My financial situation was now becoming a bit easier, as I had been asked to write the music for various radio productions and films. My wife, who had stood by me nobly throughout this difficult period, had to go into hospital at the end of 1957 for a minor operation, during which inoperable cancer was diagnosed. She died on Christmas Day.

It was fortunate in a way that I was in the midst of a

great deal of work. I had nearly finished sketching the *Variations and Finale* for the Virtuoso Ensemble and the *Symphony No. 2* which Liverpool wanted to perform in the autumn of 1958; Scherchen had asked me to write a short opera for the Berlin Festival, stipulating that it should have 'no holds barred'. I thought of Gogol's short story *The Diary of a Madman.* I adapted the libretto myself and wrote a score including electronic effects, and this was performed under Scherchen in the autumn of 1958 in Berlin. Later in 1958 I stayed with some friends in Venice and began sketching out my *Symphony No. 3* which was suggested mainly by Italian scenes. This symphony was first performed at the 1960 Edinburgh Festival by the Royal Liverpool Philharmonic Orchestra under John Pritchard. In 1960 I met my second wife, Fiona Nicholson, and we were married on 5 November that year. During 1961–2 I wrote my *Symphony No. 4,* commissioned by the Feeney Trust for the City of Birmingham Orchestra; it is characterized by a rather more fragmentary style than the earlier symphonies.

I had the idea of making Ionesco's play *The Killer* into an opera called *The Photo of the Colonel,* and this was commissioned by the BBC Third Programme as a radio opera; it was first performed by them in March 1964 and on stage at the Frankfurt Opera House in the summer of the same year. Meanwhile my wife and I had visited South Africa and it was there that I wrote a choral work, *The Song of the Sun,* for the Cheltenham Festival, based on pre-Aztec Mexican poems translated by Irene Nicholson.

While still in South Africa I had the idea of writing a fifth symphony based on certain elements of Webern's life as recounted in Friedrich Wildgans's biography, and when I returned home I found a request from the Hallé Orchestra that the first performance should be given the following October. I wrote the whole piece in three months. It was performed in Manchester under Lawrence Leonard, but by this time I was in California as composer in residence at Stanford University. In 1964 I had been invited to an opera congress at Hamburg and while there the *Intendant* of the opera house, Rolf Liebermann, asked me to write an opera for them. After rejecting various ideas I suddenly realized that *Hamlet* would make a good operatic plot; I began work on this in 1965, finishing it early in 1968. It was first performed in Hamburg in March 1968. Since then I have written a new orchestral work, *Labyrinth,* for the Royal Concert of 1971.

In writing twelve-note works I have not used classical forms to any great extent, except in the first symphony; I have tried to derive the form from the idea behind each work. I do however still use themes, which many modern composers have given up. I probably work more now with short fragments than long melodies – I have done this particularly in the fourth symphony – but I am against works being constructed entirely out of blocks of colour. My nearest to athematicism was in the opera *The Photo of the Colonel*, but there I think the basic four-note motif A-B flat-C-B natural and its inversion give one enough material to build on.

As I have said, twelve-note or indeed any kind of avant-garde music was rarely performed, and received scant appreciation in England, up to about ten years ago. Since then the position has changed considerably, however. One of the chief factors leading to this improvement was the appointment in 1959 of William Glock to the post of controller of music to the BBC. Glock was born in 1908 and was trained as a pianist; he was a pupil of Schnabel in Berlin and a critic. In 1948 he founded the Bryanston (later Dartington) School of Music, and invited avant-garde composers of all persuasions from America and Europe to expound their ideas. It was not until the BBC changed its previously conservative policy that the mass of the public in England became interested in what had been happening abroad. With Glock in charge, Schoenberg and Webern were now performed frequently, and the latest works from Donaueschingen and Darmstadt reached England without delay. In addition, young English composers were encouraged to experiment and their latest works were performed and broadcast. A further change was that a number of composers who had previously written in other styles now began to adopt the twelve-note method. The most important of these, in order of birth, are Denis ApIvor, Reginald Smith Brindle, Iain Hamilton and Alun Hoddinott.

Denis ApIvor was born in Ireland in 1916 of Welsh family. His earlier works are not particularly atonal but show a neo-romantic style and strong dramatic character. These same qualities may be found in his violin sonata of 1946 and his piano concerto of 1950. In 1952 he was commissioned, at the suggestion of Constant Lambert, to write the ballet *A Mirror for Witches* for Covent Garden, and shortly afterwards he wrote *Blood Wedding,* based on Lorca's play, for Sadler's Wells. The latter ballet has been extremely successful and was recently revived. Always a great admirer of Lorca, ApIvor has also set several of Lorca's poems as songs. His more recent works show an advanced handling of the twelve-note technique, somewhat in the manner of Webern, and include *Ubu Roi,* an opera based on the play by Alfred Jarry, which reflects his interest in the theatre of the absurd.

ApIvor has written two symphonies, of which the second dates from 1963. Other recent works are *Mutations* for cello and piano (1962), a wind quintet (1960), *Crystals* and a string quartet (both of 1964). A later work, *String Abstract,* was first performed at the 1968 Cheltenham Festival.

Reginald Smith Brindle was born in 1917 of a Yorkshire family. He entered Sicily with the invasion forces in 1943 and has lived in Italy for much of the time since then; while he was there he studied in Rome with Pizzetti and in Florence with Dallapiccola. Since 1955 his works have all employed the twelve-note method; they include *Cosmos* (1959), first performed at the 1960 Cheltenham Festival, *Concerto* for five instruments and percussion, and *Via Crucis* for string orchestra (both 1960). He has written a good deal about nodern music and published a book on serial composition, ıs well as one on contemporary percussion. His music is tough n the sense that it is well thought out intellectually and ıdmirably constructed; it also has a strong dramatic sense.

His *Amalgam* for soprano, organ and percussion, first perormed at the Cheltenham Festival of 1968, is a fusion of 'arious texts and various compositional techniques. The nusical language covers a wide area, from the present-day ıse of sound material (i.e. the use of blocks of sound, rather han notes of precise pitch) to a reworking of archaic protoypes of the early Christian era. The texts range from some y the composer himself, 'with a slight debt to Dylan 'homas and William Carlos Williams', via Gerard Manley Iopkins and the Italian mystical poetess Margherita Guidacci to the *Quid Retribuam Domino* from the Latin Mass. His *Apocalypse* for orchestra was first performed at he 1971 Cheltenham Festival. He is at present professor of nusic at the University of Bangor, North Wales.

Iain Hamilton was born in Glasgow on 6 June 1922 but ived in London from 1929 onwards. On leaving Mill Hill chool in London he was apprenticed to an engineer and emained in that profession for seven years. He had been ıaving piano lessons from the age of about ten and studied he piano when he could; when he was twenty-five he won scholarship to the Royal Academy of Music. He says that is engineering training gave him a strong sense of design nd proportion, so that form and structure in music were lways prime concerns with him.

His early works were written in a somewhat romantic liom, such as his fresh and appealing *Variations for String Orchestra,* Opus 1, of 1948, and the clarinet quintet of 1949, which is in a more melancholy vein. His first symphony, lso written in 1949, was inspired by Rostand's *Cyrano de Bergerac* and is a work full of passionate high spirits. The vork of this period shows predominantly English influences.

On leaving the Academy, Hamilton lectured on orchestraion at Morley College for several years as well as at the

University of London. He began to experiment with serial and twelve-note technique in the *Three Piano Pieces* of 1955 and the *Serenade* for clarinet and violin of the same year.

Following this period Hamilton developed in two directions simultaneously; he has always been interested in writing light music, from the comedy overture *Bartholomew Fair* of 1952 to the more recent light overture *1912* and the pot-pourri of Scottish tunes called *Écossaise*. In his more serious works, however, he has adopted the twelve-note technique in a fairly radical manner, as he has found the use of serial technique to be ultimately liberating. The composer who impressed him most in this direction was Webern with what Hamilton calls his 'superb balancing of passionate content within economic and finely controlled form. He had a magnificent sensitivity and intellect moulded with the imagination of genius'. On the other hand, Hamilton has not been greatly influenced by Stockhausen, Boulez or any of Webern's other successors.

Although in his more recent work Hamilton has not introduced new elements, he has thrown over the whole apparatus of late romantic modes of expression. This may be seen in the *Sonata for Chamber Orchestra* of 1958, where motifs are often built up from single notes, with some use of mirror-like formal construction, in the cello sonata of 1958 and in *Nocturnal* for eleven solo voices with syllables split up between the different voice parts, as in some of Nono's works. In the *Sinfonia for Two Orchestras* of 1959 short sections are interspersed with cadenza-like passages for various instrumental combinations, and there are mirror-like formations at the beginning and the end. Nevertheless in spite of the change of style, Hamilton's personality has remained constant and is clearly evident in these later works especially in the revised version (1970) of his brilliant piano concerto of ten years earlier. Since 1961 Hamilton has lived in the United States. He now divides his time between North Carolina and New York City.

Alun Hoddinott was born at Bargoed, Glamorgan, in 1929. He was educated at Gowerton Grammar School and at the University College of South Wales, Cardiff. In 1951 he was appointed lecturer in music at Cardiff College of Music and Drama; eight years later, in 1959, he became a lecturer in music at the University College of South Wales. In 1953, when he was twenty-four, he had been awarded the Walford Davies Prize for composition. His first big success came a year later when his clarinet concerto was given its first performance at the Cheltenham Festival.

His early works are written in a full-blooded romantic style and include his first two piano sonatas, a sextet, his first piano concerto and his first symphony. In recent years Hoddinott has tended more and more towards serial writing, though his music still shows the feeling for drama and colour that characterizes his tonal works.

A recent work, *Divertimenti Opus 58* for eight instruments, was written for the 1968 Cheltenham Festival; this is a light piece. His second symphony and another recent work, *Variants* for orchestra, have been recorded under the auspices of the British Council and provide an excellent introduction to his mature style. This shows a subtle and varied handling of texture and a great variety of tone colour: the big dramatic gestures of his earlier works are replaced by more economical but still striking ideas. As professor of music at Cardiff University Hoddinott has done a great deal to encourage music in Wales and to help Welsh composers to turn away from a purely provincial atmosphere and enter international musical culture.

It is outside my brief to discuss the young and very young generations of British composers, but I would like to mention briefly a few of the leading composers who have emerged during the last ten years. The oldest of this group is Thea Musgrave, a Scottish composer who, in spite of studying for four years in Paris with Nadia Boulanger, has not been influenced by neo-classicism; on the contrary, she has absorbed serial technique and every new musical discovery of recent times. Her intentions are clear and her line direct; among her works is the *Triptych* for tenor and orchestra of 1959 which has a decisively personal note, in spite of possible debts to earlier composers. Her recent opera, *The Decision*, was a great success when it was given a few performances at Sadler's Wells. She has also written a considerable amount of chamber music, including two piano sonatas, a violin sonata and a string quartet. Her *Obliques* were first performed in Glasgow in 1961 to a packed house. Her full-length ballet, *Beauty and the Beast*, was produced with success by the Scottish Theatre Ballet, and she has recently written two concertos, the first of which, for clarinet and orchestra, requires the soloist to perambulate through the orchestra and play with different groups of instrumentalists from time to time, creating a stereophonic effect. In the second (1971), for horn and orchestra, the four orchestral horn players surround the soloist at one point and engage in a kind of parodistic battle with him.

The next three composers form the so-called Manchester Group, which consists of Alexander Goehr, Peter Maxwell Davies and Harrison Birtwistle. They were all students in Manchester at the same time and, together with the pianist John Ogdon, formed a performing group which brought their music to London in 1956.

Alexander Goehr, born in 1932, is the son of Walter Goehr. Already his earlier works, such as the *Fantasias for Clarinet and Piano* (1952) and the *Fantasia for Orchestra* (1954) showed him to be well at home in the avant-garde style of the day. In 1955–6 he spent a year at the Paris Conservatoire, studying with Messiaen and his wife, Yvonne Loriod. Like the other composers of this group, Goehr accepted the serial heritage as a matter of course. Though he professes a great respect for Schoenberg, he is equally likely to be influenced by Beethoven or Boulez. He himself feels that he has learnt a good deal from Webern in the technical field and that he follows Schoenberg when he s faced with a dramatic conflict between the series and the raditional motivic structure of music.

The work which first made Goehr well-known was *The)eluge,* a cantata written in 1957–8. This is a highly expres-ive, violent and picturesque piece. Another cantata, *Sutter's Gold,* dealing with the discovery of the Californian gold-ields, was commissioned by the Leeds Festival of 1961, but he performers failed to understand the piece and the work ias not yet received an adequate performance. In some later vorks, such as the violin concerto and the *Little Symphony,* Goehr has judged his means surely and produced music vhich can be readily appreciated. He undoubtedly wishes iis music to be understood and his forms become clearer vith each piece. One could say that he takes Schoenberg .s his starting point and develops his own style from there; t is not avant-garde in the sense that the music of some of iis contemporaries is, but it is full of ingenious ideas and .t the same time is solidly constructed. He has recently vritten three music theatre works, which are given in a oncert hall, but with a certain amount of acting, mime, inging, dancing and lighting, accompanied by a small in-trumental ensemble. These three works, *Naboth's Vineyard, Shadowplay* and *Sonata about Jerusalem,* amount to minia-ure operas and are of course easier to stage than full-scale lramatic works.

For some years Goehr took a regular class at Morley College and from 1960 until 1967 he held a part-time job .t the BBC, being responsible for the production of orches-ral concerts. His opera, *Arden Muss Sterben,* with a libretto y Erich Fried, was commissioned by the Hamburg State)pera and first performed there in 1967. This is a black omedy based on the seventeenth-century English play *Arden of Faversham*; the staging has certain Brechtian choes, but the music does not attempt to parody Kurt Veill – it is in Goehr's natural style with some additional ouches of humour.

Peter Maxwell Davies was born in Manchester on 8

September 1934 and educated at Leigh Grammar School before going to the Royal Manchester College of Music anc Manchester University. In 1957 he won an Italian govern ment scholarship and went to Rome to study with Petrassi While in Rome he wrote his *Prolation* for orchestra, whicl won the 1959 Olivetti Prize and was performed at th ISCM festival in that same year. His early works are exu berant and fantastic, as may be seen in the *Fantasias fo Clarinet and Piano* of 1956 and the *Capriccio* for piano o 1957. His *St Michael Sonata* for seventeen wind instru ments derives its basic material from the chants of th Requiem Mass and shows his interest in mediæval music an interest which has increased with time. From 1959 t 1962 Maxwell Davies was director of music at Cirenceste Grammar School, where he was able to make schoolchildre perform music of a very avant-garde character, often writin pieces for them himself, and greatly stimulating their in terest in music. While there he composed two works i which children take part: *O Magnum Mysterium* and *T Lucis ante Terminum,* cycles of carols with instrumenta sonatas. Other works show his interest in mediæval music such as the use of a Dunstable motet in the sextet *Alm Redemptoris Mater* (1957) and a mediæval carol in *Ricerca and Doubles* (1959). These works combine certain tech niques of mediæval music with those of contemporar Continental practice. Davies has said that he has a 'certai nostalgia for the mediæval period, where life had a ver deep level of meaning and symbolism, without being in th least self-conscious'. In 1962 the first of his two fantasias o an *In Nomine* of John Taverner, commissioned by the BBC was performed at a Prom concert and won a prize at a International Music Council contest for compositions. In th same year he was given a Harkness Fellowship and wen for further study to the Graduate Music School at Princeto University.

In recent years he has written several music theatr works, such as his *Eight Songs for a Mad King* with it

17 A photograph of the author (b. 1915) taken in 1960.

18 Priaulx Rainier (b. 1903), a South African composer resident in England.

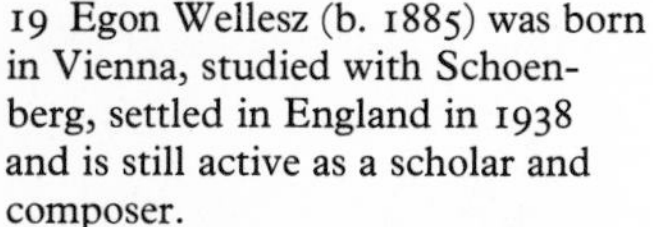

19 Egon Wellesz (b. 1885) was born in Vienna, studied with Schoenberg, settled in England in 1938 and is still active as a scholar and composer.

20 Elisabeth Lutyens (b. 1906), a commanding figure among England's women composers.

21 The Manchester School in 1956. Left to right: (front row) Alexander Goehr, Audrey Goehr, John Dow, (back row) Harrison Birtwistle, John Ogdon, Elgar Howarth, Peter Maxwell Davies.
22 Richard Rodney Bennett (b. 1936) studied with Boulez and attracted attention early through his rapid mastery of the technique of serial writing.
23 Peter Racine Fricker (b. 1920) numbers Jean Racine among his ancestors but grew up in England. Much of his music shows the influence of Bartók through his teacher Mátyás Seiber.
24 Roberto Gerhard (1896–1970), a Spanish composer who came to live in Cambridge and worked extensively with *musique concrète* and electronic music.

25 Henk Badings (b. 1907), a prolific Dutch composer who has made tonal and harmonic experiments along original lines.

26 Willem Pijper (1894–1947), the best-known Dutch composer of recent times as well as an energetic teacher and organiser.

27 Guillaume Landré (1905–1968), Willem Pijper's foremost pupil.

28 Ton de Leeuw (b. 1926) and his family; with Henk Badings he has been instrumental in Holland's development as a centre for electronic music.

29 Louis Andriessen (b. 1939) photographed in 1970: the avant-garde son of a family of Dutch composers.

performers in gilded cages; *Revelation and Fall,* a setting of a poem by Georg Trakl which uses amplification of the instruments through loudspeakers and of the voice through a loud-hailer with a number of unusually large percussion instruments and the ensemble arranged in the form of a cross; and *Vesalii Icones,* a work for solo dancer and instrumental ensemble based on Vesalius' anatomical drawings and also related to the Stations of the Cross. To perform these works, Maxwell Davies formed his own group, formerly the Pierrot Players, now renamed The Fires of London, and he writes almost exclusively for them.

The third composer of this group, Harrison Birtwistle, was born in 1934. His works, on the whole smaller in scale than those of Goehr or Davies, express a private, rather haunting world. They include *Refrains and Choruses* for wind quintet, *Music for Sleep* for child singers and instrumentalists and a *Tragœdia* for ten players in which the wind instruments also play claves. A recent work is the opera *Punch and Judy,* performed at the Aldeburgh Festival of 1968; while showing a violent and original approach to the problems of modern opera, it certainly does not attempt to revive the romantic opera in new circumstances; the action is interrupted by extraneous events such as games and weather forecasts. Birtwistle has also written several instrumental works for The Fires of London, including *Medusa,* an extended work which seems to present every possibility of the use of the semitone. At the time of writing he is working on a new full-length opera for Covent Garden.

Richard Rodney Bennett, born in 1936, studied at the Royal Academy with Howard Ferguson, privately with Elisabeth Lutyens and in Paris with Boulez. He developed very early and was able to assimilate both knowledge and style from an early age. Some of his early works combine late romantic ideas with the influence of Bartók. His work with Boulez gave him an easy command of total serialization, and since 1959 he has produced a large number of pieces, all of them attractive in sound, effortless in technique and extremely well written. He has been writing film scores since 1955, when he was only nineteen, but his large output has not led to a facile technique. His opera *The Mines of Sulphur* and the one-act opera, *The Ledge,* show a genuine dramatic gift. His opera *Victory,* based on Joseph Conrad's novel, was produced at Covent Garden in 1970; it is effectively dramatic and was successful with the London audience. Bennett's style is not so radical as that of Maxwell Davies or Birtwistle, but he is a fluent and ingenious composer, as may be seen in his recent piano concerto.

Another Royal Academy student, Cornelius Cardew, born in 1936, went to Cologne and worked with Stockhausen. He has been concerned mainly with graphic and experimental notation and with indeterminate or partly determined composition. He represents the real avant-garde in this country in the international sense. Cardew was the most radical composer to use the principle of indeterminacy and in this he has been followed by a number of the younger composers of today. Goehr and Maxwell Davies have been against this principle, though in Maxwell Davies's string quartet the individual players are allowed to set their own speed for melismata in specified places, while the tempo of the main part remains fixed; in certain educational pieces Davies has also left places free for improvisation but always on given material, and the improvisation must be coherent. For such performances Davies supervises the rehearsals and encourages the players to express themselves coherently in musical terms. In general, indeterminate or aleatoric music, very common on the Continent, has not really taken root in this country. There are of course a number of composers younger than Bennett and Cardew who are working with advanced techniques and obtaining quite a number of performances, but it is too early to comment on them in this volume. The most notable of these appear to be David Bedford, Roger Smalley and John Tavener.

The lighter side of English music today is chiefly represented by Malcolm Arnold and Malcolm Williamson. Malcolm Arnold, born in 1921, studied with Gordon Jacob at the Royal College and became principal trumpet in the London Philharmonic Orchestra; he thus knows the orchestra from the inside and his handling of it is invariably brilliant. He has produced a number of excitingly written scores of which I might mention his *English Dances* and his later *Scottish* and *Cornish Dances,* as well as several ballets, including *Homage to the Queen* and *Rinaldo and Armida,* six symphonies, of which the last is partly written in a jazz idiom, several sinfoniettas, numerous concertos and many other works. He has said himself that he aims only to write light music, but in fact his music often has a serious quality. Malcolm Arnold does not consider the present day symphony orchestra out of date, and he feels that if it must be augmented, it would be better to add instruments to the extreme registers – flutes, piccolos, E flat clarinet or contra-bassoon. He works quickly, revising very little, and never uses a piano in composing. He prefers to remain within the diatonic system, believing that it affords the best opportunity for creating musical ideas; atonal music leads, he says, to a state of musical meandering. In spite of his great success with orchestral music, he considers a string quartet the best work he has ever written.

Malcolm Williamson was born in Australia in 1931 and studied at the Sydney Conservatorium under Eugene Goossens. He came to Europe to work with Elisabeth Lutyens and he also encountered Boulez. Since 1953 he has been living in England, where he undertook further study with Elisabeth Lutyens and Erwin Stein. He is an extremely eclectic composer who has written in a dozen different styles, ranging from strict serialism to pop tunes of the Richard Rodgers type. Often one finds the night-club pianist and the Catholic organist within one piece, or at any rate in pieces written at the same time. His opera, *English Eccentrics,* of 1964, with words by Edith Sitwell, is a kind of diversion showing all his different strains: witty, exuberant, high-spirited, melancholy, devout and visionary. Other operas include *Our Man in Havana*, *Julius Caesar Jones* and *The Violins of Saint-Jacques*. He has also written orchestral music, string quartets, piano and organ pieces and Roman Catholic church music in a modern pop-song style.

7 Willem Pijper and music in Holland

The history of music in Holland is in many ways similar to that of England. In the fifteenth and sixteenth centuries the so-called Netherlands composers laid the foundations of Western European polyphony. Unlike Germany and Italy, Holland did not have princely courts which attracted orchestras and artists and, as the Calvinist religion predominated, there was little demand for music in religious services. During the seventeenth and eighteenth centuries there were a number of composers resident in Holland who did not achieve international fame but wrote music of a high standard. Dutch national music did not really begin to emerge until Holland became independent in 1830.

German influence on Dutch music was extremely strong throughout the nineteenth century; the first markedly nationalist Dutch composer, Bernard Zweers (1854–1924), studied in Leipzig but insisted on using Dutch texts for all his work.

The first Dutch composer to become established internationally was Alphons Diepenbrock (1862–1921). His first major work was the *Missa in die Festo* of 1894. In his early days he had admired Wagner greatly, but in 1910 came under the influence of Debussy and the French school. He set a number of the German romantic poets – Goethe,

Hölderlin, Brentano and Novalis – chiefly with orchestral accompaniment; but he also set a number of late nineteenth-century French poets, such as Baudelaire, Verlaine and Laforgue. His Verlaine settings can be favourably compared with those of Fauré or Debussy.

Diepenbrock was mostly self-taught. His exact contemporary, Johan Wagenaar (1862–1941) was a thoroughly professional musician. It can be said that on the one hand the foundations of modern Dutch music were laid by the inspired fantasy of Diepenbrock, and on the other by the solid technique of Wagenaar.

The next generation of Dutch composers began to throw off the German domination which had lasted so long in Holland, and to turn more in the direction of French music. After the First World War, a number of modern composers in Holland formed a Society for Modern Creative Music. One of these was Matthijs Vermeulen (1888–1967). Though Vermeulen's work was at first reasonably successful, his *Symphony No. 2* was refused performance by Mengelberg, the conductor of the Concertgebouw Orchestra, as being too avant-garde. It used an atonal, polymelodic manner of writing, for which there was no example at that time in Holland. The rebuff disappointed Vermeulen so deeply that he went to live in France, and did not return to Holland until 1947. After the war Vermeulen received much greater appreciation in Holland; his *Symphony No. 2* was performed for the first time in that country at the Holland Festival of 1956 and, encouraged, he wrote several more symphonies which were performed with success.

However, the most important Dutch composer of this generation, and one who was to become really well-known internationally, was Willem Pijper (1894–1947). He was born in the village of Zeist, near Utrecht. His family held strict Calvinist views, and music was hardly to be heard in the household. His health was so poor that he was unable to go to school, and being an only child he was thrown very much on his own resources. His first musical discoveries consisted of collecting together on the harmonium all sorts of sounds and building up his own sound system. Apart from his interest in music, he also showed a great interest in plants and animals, and he was fascinated by biology for the rest of his life; this ties up with the 'germ-cell theory' which he was to develop as a composer.

In these years he read a great deal and when he eventually went to school at the age of fourteen he was far ahead of the other pupils in general education. When he was seventeen he studied composition with Johan Wagenaar at the Utrecht Conservatoire. Wagenaar did not stand in his way when he wanted to carry out experimental work. Even in an early work such as the first string quartet of 1914, there are bitonal moments, with, for instance, E flat minor and C minor appearing together; Pijper had thought out these effects entirely on his own. The musical portraits which he made for fun also contain polytonal complexes which were well ahead of their time.

The two composers who chiefly influenced Pijper after his period of study at the Conservatoire were Debussy and Mahler. Pijper wrote a song cycle for voice and orchestra, *Fêtes Galantes* (1916), to poems by Verlaine, showing a Debussyan influence, and also his first symphony, entitled *Pan* (1917), which has more in common with Mahler, being written for a large orchestra with elaborate percussion. But whereas in Mahler's work one feels that man is involved with nature, Pijper's *Nature Symphony* contains no human figures; it shows more of a heathen, animistic feeling for the genius of nature. After leaving the Conservatoire, Pijper became music critic of the *Utrechtsch Dagblad*, and later directed the Utrecht Sextet.

By 1918 his development as a composer was more or less complete. He broke away more and more from the shackles of the bar line, using polymetric and polyrhythmic figures. He also used bitonality and polytonality to an increasing extent; he was a staunch opponent of Schoenberg's atonality, which he regarded as a destructive force. His *Piano Sona-*

tina No. 3 of 1925, for instance, begins with a complex based on two keys a tritone apart, this being the constructive element of the whole piece. Again, the first chord of his *Piano Concerto* of 1927 is a combination of two three-note chords belonging to different keys; this kind of 'germ-cell' provides the basis for the whole work.

Pijper's work again developed between 1919 and 1926. His first violin sonata and first cello sonata (both 1919) are still mainly tonal, though there are polytonal elements and also polyrhythms in places. The *Septet* for five wind instruments, double bass and piano of 1920 is constructed on the germ-cell principle, and Pijper reached complete maturity in his second string quartet (1920), the second piano trio (1921), the second violin sonata (1922) and the third string quartet (1923). His important second symphony was written at Lake Maggiore in 1921 and first performed by Mengelberg at the Concertgebouw in November of 1922.

Pijper's best-known work, the *Symphony No. 3,* was written in 1926; it was dedicated to his friend Pierre Monteux, who performed it throughout the world. The whole symphony is based on a germ-cell of three notes and two rhythmic motifs; it is in one movement which combines all the elements of the classical symphony. As a motto in the score he copied a line from Virgil: *Flectere si nequeo superos, Acheronta movebo* (*If I cannot bend the powers above I will move those below*). Ths would appear to refer to Orpheus, who, by his playing, was able to tame wild animals and move stones, and the third symphony is certainly one of Pijper's most convincing and impressive works.

In 1928 Pijper was commissioned to write a work for the fortieth anniversary of the founding of the Concertgebouw Orchestra: this was his *Symphonic Epigrams,* six short pieces based on a single motif, an old Dutch song, 'O Netherlands, heed thy cause'. It was intended as a rallying-cry to Dutch musicians to take a stand for their own creative work. In 1930 Pijper was appointed director of the Rotterdam Conservatoire, and shortly afterwards wrote the opera

Halewijn. He described it both as a 'symphonic drama', meaning that the form and tension of the action are determined solely and completely by the music, and as a 'visually perceptible symphony'. Its thematic material derives from the old folk tune to which the ballad of Halewijn was sung in the middle ages.

His work for the theatre included incidental music for Shakespeare's *The Tempest.* His later works include a violin concerto, a cello concerto and a sonata for solo violin. The first movement of the *Violin Concerto* combines two different tempi; the orchestra moves in slow crotchets, while the solo violin part proceeds in fairly rapid quavers. Pijper died on 19 March 1947 at the age of only fifty-three. His early death was a serious loss to Dutch musical life, and it was especially unfortunate that he was not able to experience the renewal of cultural life in Holland after the wartime Nazi occupation.

Though Pijper's life was uneventful on the whole, we can get some idea of his character from a memorial address given shortly after his death by his pupil Bertus Van Lier:

> The summary characteristic seems to me to lie in Pijper's subtle sensitivity to what is ephemeral, in a sensitivity to the moment that does not return. He felt the sanctity, the uniqueness of the moment so dynamically and violently that what was momentary, ephemeral and fleeting was for him the symbol of the immutable. He had a Latin, typically French spirit which was sensitive to southern dance rhythms and he loathed all heaviness. . . . The germ-cell became for him the symbol of the everlasting principle of which all that is transitory is a manifestation. We recognize in this the grammar school pupil whose main love was botany. I still remember well the large box divided into compartments covered with a glass plate in which seeds of various types were arranged; he always kept that box, the box with the germ-cell, until German forces destroyed that house with all Rotterdam. We also recognise in this the later Willem Pijper, who found the same idea both in modern psychiatry and ancient Greek tragedy, the idea that the behaviour of man is determined by germ-cells, planted in the soil of the child's soul, which subsequently govern his life logically and illogically.

He had to turn against all stabilising and stagnating cults, against the innumerably repeated use and abuse of melodies which were once virgin, against small holy edifices and the deification of systems. This was often viewed as a mere pursuit of originality. Unjustifiably so, since he knew that the truly creative reveals itself in the moment which does not return.

8 Dutch composers since 1945

When Dutch cultural life revived after the end of the German occupation in 1945 the composers who came to the fore were mainly pupils of Willem Pijper. Among the most important of these was Guillaume Landré (1905–1968). Before the war he had attracted attention with a symphony (1932), a suite for string orchestra and piano (1936), and a short opera, *The Pike* (1937). His earlier works were strongly influenced by Pijper, but instead of working with the short, concentrated 'germ-cell' motifs characteristic of Pijper, Landré tended to use longer, more lyrical melodies. Many of his works are elegiac, a good example being the slow central movement of the *String Orchestra Suite*. The same elegiac mood is a feature of other pieces such as the *Piae Memoriae pro patria mortuorum* for chorus, trumpet and orchestra; and the *Symphony No. 3*, dedicated to the memory of a friend. This last work is typical of Landré's methods, in that the slow introduction states a basic theme from which most of the thematic material of the work is derived.

The same procedure may be traced in the *Symphony No. 4*; it is constructed round one basic motif, which is stated at the opening by the brass and returns in each of the five movements in various forms, though it is not fully developed until the finale. In this work, the full orchestra is used only in the first and last movements, the middle movements being scored for strings and harp, woodwind and horns, and brass and percussion respectively. His *Kaleidoscope* of 1956 is based on a short motif followed by a series of chords: this material is varied during the work, which after a dramatic climax ends in a mood of reverie. Later works by Landré, such as the *Permutazione sinfoniche* and *Anagrams,* show a dodecaphonic structure of a kind, though they are not strictly based on the twelve-note technique. Landré wrote a fairly large number of other orchestral works which were frequently performed both in Holland and abroad. He will be remembered as a composer who did a great deal to revive Dutch music in the post-war years.

If Landré's music looks back to Pijper and the romantic past to some extent, another of Pijper's pupils, Kees van Baaren, born in 1906, is far more forward-looking. Van Baaren studied at the Berlin Hochschule für Musik as well as with Pijper, and at an early age was strongly attracted by the music of the Second Viennese School. Serial technique appears in his *Wind Trio* of 1936. Never a doctrinaire composer, he has experimented with various methods of musical expression in order to find those which will suit him best. After a cantata based on T. S. Eliot's *The Hollow Men* (1948), Van Baaren wrote a *Septet* for violin, double bass and wind quintet in 1952, the first Dutch work in which the twelve-note technique is used consistently. His symphony, written for a Haydn-sized orchestra, and his *Variazioni per orchestra* of 1959 also use serial technique. In the latter work, the variations successively treat vertical note-groups, interval-relations, and variable groupings as regards metre and length of notes. Two more recent works, *Sovrapozione I* for string quartet and *Sovrapozione II* for wind quintet superimpose six twelve-note series and contain sections in which completely different tempi and structures of different character overlap simultaneously; there is also some use of aleatoric principles. Since 1957 Van Baaren has been the director of the Royal Conservatory in The Hague, where he has taught most of the younger generation of Dutch experimental composers. Though he has never attempted to influence his pupils in their choice of style, his own work in the field of serial and post-serial writing has made him an invaluable guide for younger composers, and his compositions, if few in number, have made a notable and original contribution to Dutch music.

Another pupil of Pijper who has achieved international recognition is Henk Badings, born in 1907 at Bandoeng in Java, where his father was an administrative officer. His parents died when he was still young, and he came to Holland at the age of eight. His guardian would not allow him to have a musical education, and he was sent to study engineering at the Delft Technical University, graduating with honours in 1931. His special interest was geology, and he worked for a few years as an assistant in the laboratory of palæontology and geology at Delft University, visiting several European countries while doing scientific research, but spending all his spare time in musical studies. He was largely self-taught. While still studying engineering he sat for a composition examination which was adjudicated by Pijper, who then accepted him as a pupil and encouraged him to write his first symphony. Badings submitted this work for a competition in Amsterdam and it won the first prize; its subsequent performance by the Concertgebouw brought his name before the public. Badings did not study for long with Pijper, however, chiefly because their outlook differed.

His second symphony was taken up by the young Eduard van Beinum, to whom it was dedicated, and who performed it with the Concertgebouw orchestra all over the world. Since then Badings has written an enormous number of works; a catalogue published in 1966 lists more than three hundred and twenty-five, including twelve symphonies, twenty concertos, twenty-one symphonic works of various kinds, six operas, forty-six chamber music works and a large number of songs and choral works. In general he may be said to follow the Brahms-Reger-Hindemith tradition; many of his compositions are elaborately contrapuntal. His earlier works, those written up to 1940, are sombre and elegiac in character, while his later ones are lighter in tone and more transparent in orchestration; though he has played with bi- and polytonality, his music usually has a tonal centre. He has also experimented with six- and seven-note series which suggest a combination of Lydian and Mixolydian modalities, and has built up a harmonic system on a scale consisting of alternate major and minor seconds. He is interested in the problem of tuning and wrote a number of works for Professor A. D. Fokker's thirty-one-keyed organ in the Teyler Museum in Haarlem; his experimental *Contrasts* for unaccompanied chorus makes the singers use pure tuning.

Badings has also experimented in other ways: his *Orpheus and Eurydice* (1941), for instance, is a four-act dramatic ballet in which Eurydice is a dancer, Orpheus an actor, and there is a large part for a solo baritone. Since 1952 he has been interested in electronic music, his first large work in this medium being the radio opera *Orestes,* which won the Italia Prize in 1954. In this he represented the Erinnyes by a speeded-up recording of a male chorus; the score in fact is *musique concrète* rather than real electronic music, since it is based on distortions of musical or natural sounds. Badings did use electronic sounds in his ballet *Cain and Abel,* made at the Philips studio in Eindhoven, but they are combined with traditional motifs in 'pure' tuning. He used the same technique in another radio opera, *Asterion,* commissioned by the South African Radio Corporation, but his television opera *Salto Mortale* of 1957 is accompanied solely by electronic music. Badings has also experimented with computers in recent years, and some of his purely orchestral works, such as the later symphonies, contain 'electronic' sounds produced by orchestral means. Apart from being a prolific composer, Badings still finds time for teaching; since 1951 he has taught acoustics in the

Musicological Institute at Utrecht State University, and since 1962 has been professor of composition at the Stuttgart Universität für Musik, as well as being guest professor at the University of Adelaide from 1962 to 1963.

Some of the younger generation of Dutch composers also deserve mention. Ton de Leeuw, born in 1926, intended to study with Pijper but on the latter's death went first to Badings and then to Messiaen in Paris. He has experimented with problems of rhythm and sonority, as in his *Mouvements rétrogrades* of 1957, while his *String Quartet No. 1* of 1958 is influenced by serial technique. As sound director of the Netherlands Radio from 1954 onwards he was able to use radiophonic techniques, especially in his oratorio *Job*, which won the Italia Prize. Here radiophonic effects are combined with 'normal' music. His interest in unusual rhythms led him to study African and oriental music; this influenced his music for the piano, such as the *Four Rhythmic Studies* and the *Three African Studies*, his orchestral works *Ombres* and *Nritta,* the opera *The Dream*, and the *Haiku* songs. Recently he has been using a proportional notation in which the duration of each note is represented by the distances between the individual notes on the paper: thus the music is measured by time rather than in the conventional manner, a practice which a good many composers have adopted these days. Ton de Leeuw first used this method of notation in a *Symphony for Wind Instruments* commissioned by the Pittsburgh Wind Symphony Orchestra in 1963.

The avant-garde in Holland is chiefly represented by Peter Schat, born in 1935, and Louis Andriessen, born in 1939. Peter Schat first became prominent in the late fifties, with his *Septet* for wind, cello, piano and percussion, a twelve-note work which scored a success at the 1950 Strasbourg ISCM festival. He followed this with *Mosaics* for orchestra (1959), *Entelechy* for five groups of instruments (1961), and *Signalement* for six percussion instruments and three double basses (1962). His *Improvisations* and

Symphonies (1962) for wind quintet contain aleatory and improvisational elements. Schat had studied in Holland with Kees van Baaren, as well as in London with Mátyás Seiber and in Basle with Pierre Boulez. His most sensational success came with the production of his *Labyrinth* at the 1966 Holland Festival; this took the form of a piece of 'total theatre' in which Schat collaborated with a team of other young artists – a writer, a choreographer, a film-maker, a costume designer, an architect and scene-designer and a stage director. The dramatic story is constantly interrupted, not only by an 'old woman' appearing in various guises, but by three vocal soloists, who chant an entirely different plot in Latin, and by film sequences and dances. The music for the dances is purely orchestral – the orchestra contains no violins, but a large number of bass instruments – and there are also incantations for chorus and orchestra, improvisations for the three singers and four instrumental soloists, and electronic music. The chorus sits among the spectators during the first two acts, then climbs on to the stage in the third at the command of the old woman: at the end of the work they destroy the labyrinth. In a more recent work, *On Escalation* (1968) six percussion players are each surrounded by a small group of other instruments to which they give instructions with reference to the main conductor, and then gradually withdraw from his influence as the piece proceeds. The form is that of a continuous crescendo achieved by controlled improvisation and contains a number of quotations from other composers, including Ravel (*Bolero*) and Palestrina.

Louis Andriessen, the youngest son of the veteran Dutch composer Hendrik Andriessen, was taught by his father and Kees van Baaren, and later by Luciano Berio. He first attracted attention with his *Nocturnes* for soprano and orchestra and three pieces called *Introspezione*. His *Anachrony I* of 1967, which is dedicated to the memory of Charles Ives, shows in places a Stravinsky-like use of material written by other composers. It is scored for normal orchestra, with the celesta, piano and electronic organ arranged in a central position round the conductor: the whole work is based on a four-note phrase which suggests a 6/4 chord and thus gives a hint of tonality. There are quotations from Roussel's third symphony and Bach's *St Matthew Passion,* as well as other passages in a strictly serial style. As one critic wrote: 'The score indicates more than clearly that an individual style is no longer the ideal'. A more recent work, *Contra Tempus* (1968) contains fewer quotations, but there are reminiscences of Andriessen's own *Introspezione III* and the Mass of Guillaume de Machaut – the fact that the series contains major and minor chords facilitates the link with Machaut's language. The work is scored for groups of individual instruments – four keyboard instruments, including electronic tapes, three trombones, four violas, woodwind without clarinets, and percussion.

Electronic music has been extensively cultivated in Holland. To make Varèse's *Poème Electronique* for the 1958 Brussels Exhibition, a special studio was constructed by the firm of Philips in Eindhoven, and Badings and other Dutch composers have worked there. A second studio was set up temporarily in the Technical University in Delft in 1957, where a number of other composers also worked. In 1960 all the equipment was centralized in a large studio in Utrecht University and Badings took charge of it.

9 The great Scandinavian symphonists - Sibelius and Nielsen

When Jean Sibelius and Carl Nielsen were born in 1865, the only Scandinavian composer with an international reputation was the Dane, Niels Gade, whose Mendelssohnian symphonies enjoyed a certain following in Germany. Grieg and Svendsen were still in their twenties and on the threshold of their careers; in Sweden, Berwald was nearing the end of his life without having achieved the recognition that was his due. His masterpiece, the *Sinfonie singulière*, did not receive its first performance until the present century and his fame did not penetrate outside Sweden until the late 1940's. In Finland the dominant musical influences were German and no composer of importance had emerged.

Sibelius was born on 8 December 1865 at Hämeenlinna, a small town in south-central Finland. His father was a doctor and senior physician to the local territorial battalion, and his mother's family was of mixed Swedish and Finnish origin. Sibelius's father died when he was only two-and-a-half, and the family then lived with Sibelius's grandmother. Sibelius's uncle was a keen amateur violinist, with whom Sibelius often stayed.

He acquired the Christian name by which he is internationally known from one of his other uncles, Johan, who used the Gallicized form of the name when abroad. When as a young man he discovered a set of visiting cards belonging to his late uncle, he followed his example and adopted the name for the rest of his life.

At the age of twenty he left for Helsinki to start his university studies; his family had decided that he should read law to equip himself for an official career. He also enrolled at the Music Institute where he continued his violin studies; he still cherished ambitions to become a solo violinist and during these years developed a more than respectable technique. It was evident after a time that his law studies were not prospering and that music was to be his life. He became a pupil of Martin Wegelius, who not only gave him a thorough grounding of theoretical instruction but became a great friend too. Wegelius was a devoted Wagnerian, an attitude that his young pupil did not share; Sibelius's enthusiasms were for Tchaikovsky and Grieg. Sibelius continued to compose and towards the end of his student years Wegelius offered him a good deal of encouragement. A suite for string trio and a quartet were both given at a Music Institute concert. Also on the staff for a time was Busoni, though he was a year younger than Sibelius, and the two became life-long friends. In later years Busoni championed Sibelius's work, including the *Symphony No. 2*, in his New Music concerts.

In September 1889 Sibelius set out for Berlin, having been awarded a small scholarship to further his studies. On Wegelius's recommendation he went to Albert Becker, a highly academic figure with whom he embarked on a study of strict counterpoint and fugue.

In Berlin Strauss's *Don Juan* was among the new music he heard under Hans von Bülow's baton and he also attended von Bülow's Beethoven sonata recitals and the Joachim quartet's performances of late Beethoven. And yet Berlin was not the stimulating musical centre it was to become in later years, and its Prussian atmosphere was not congenial to him.

While pursuing his studies with Becker, Sibelius wrote relatively little; the only work of note is the G minor *Piano Quintet*, inspired partly by Christian Sinding's essay in this medium. During this year Robert Kajanus came to Berlin and conducted a performance of his *Aino Symphony,* which gave Sibelius a decisive impulse to turn to the Finnish national epic, the *Kalevala,* for the inspiration of his first major orchestral work, the *Kullervo Symphony.*

In the autumn of 1890 Sibelius embarked on another year of foreign study, this time in Vienna. He arrived armed with a letter of recommendation from Busoni to Brahms, but the latter declined to meet him and Sibelius finally chose to study with Robert Fuchs and the composer Goldmark, then at the height of his fame. He had few lessons from him, as Goldmark was far too busy to teach him on a regular basis, but he did give him encouragement and help in finding his orchestral feet. In Vienna Sibelius made the first drafts of the *Kullervo Symphony* and also worked on an octet which probably provided the material for *En Saga.* Sibelius found Vienna far more to his taste than Berlin; he heard Johann Strauss conduct his own waltzes and took a liking for them which lasted all his life. He also met a number of celebrities in the salons of the singer Pauline Lucca.

Sibelius returned to Finland in the summer of 1891 and the *Kullervo Symphony* had its premiere the following April. This was the first major symphonic work by an indigenous composer; its proportions were ambitious, indeed positively Mahlerian, and in it Sibelius sounded the call of Finnish nationalism which inevitably set off a responsive chord in a country whose national self-consciousness was slowly but surely emerging. Not only was this work a tremendous success but it marks the emergence of a distinctive individual voice in Scandinavian music. From the very first bars there is no doubt of its authorship, and even though the symphony does not achieve the level of mastery of the mature symphonies, it has much of the epic sweep we associate with Sibelius.

Kullervo shows us the path Sibelius chose not to follow: that of the vast programmatic canvas. Its central movement, the quasi-operatic scene *Kullervo and his sister*, reveals something of his dramatic talent. The vocal writing is highly effective and the feeling for atmosphere strong, but his dramatic characterization does not reach the standard found in great opera. The two operatic ventures that he pursued in the 1890s, *The Building of the Boat* and the *Maiden in the Tower*, failed to prosper not only on this count but because of his inability to come to terms with Wagner.

After the success of *Kullervo,* Kajanus commissioned a repertoire piece from him and the result was *En Saga* (1893), but this was not the success he had expected and *En Saga* as we know it is the revision made in 1901. This and the *Karelia* music serve to establish his credentials as a nationalist and by far the most gifted composer Finland has produced. But perhaps it is the *Lemminkäinen Suite* (1895) that most effectively encapsulates the spirit of the *Kalevala.* Its most famous movement, *The Swan of Tuonela,* was originally the prelude to *The Building of the Boat,* and it is possible that some of the other ideas in the suite originally come from the opera. Sibelius was struggling with both works during his visit to Bayreuth in 1894 and when he finally abandoned the opera it was, according to the composer's most recent biographer, Erik Tawaststjerna, the result of his encounter with Wagner's operas. Sibelius's brother-in-law Armas Järnefelt, the conductor, and composer of a well-known *Praeludium,* was a fervent Wagnerite and dragged Sibelius off to Bayreuth for the summer so as to add another convert to the cause (Sibelius had married Aino Järnefelt in June 1892). But it was the symphonic poem rather than the operatic stage that conquered; and the *Lemminkäinen Suite* (or *Four Legends*) was the next landmark in Sibelius's creative career. In terms of imaginative mastery they represent a giant step forward in the forging of his individual musical language.

After *Kullervo,* Sibelius had mainly made his living by

teaching, but recognition of his talent was growing, and in 1897 the Finnish senate granted him a small life-pension which relieved him of some of his teaching obligations.

In 1898 after writing music for Adolf Paul's play, *King Christian II,* he found a continental publisher, Breitkopf and Härtel. He had, alas, little business sense, and *Valse triste,* which should have earned him a fortune, was sold outright for a pittance of three hundred marks, a decision that haunted the rest of his days. But it is a mark of his achievement that the State pension given him should have preceded his first symphony, just as it is a measure of the seriousness with which he addressed himself to the symphonic discipline that he should have waited until his mid-thirties to test his symphonic powers.

Thus the first symphony is a landmark in his career. His previous orchestral works had been either narrative or descriptive, and this was his first major abstract work; it is on the seven symphonies that his reputation rightly rests. But for his countrymen his reputation at this time rested on the patriotic music and above all the last of the *Historic Tableaux* he composed in 1899 for the press celebrations. Because of increasing pressure from the occupying power, national feeling was rising and *Finlandia,* as this movement came to be known, was the rallying-point for Finnish patriotic sentiment. Music was harnessed in the national cause: Europe was made aware of Finnish aspirations and Kajanus led the Helsinki Orchestra on a tour of Northern Europe, Germany and France that was as much intended to focus attention on Finland as an oppressed country as it was to promote composers like Sibelius and Järnefelt.

After this tour Sibelius repaired to Italy, for which he had a life-long passion, and it was in Rapallo that the second symphony came into being. Italy, incidentally, was the unlikely home for him during the composition of his least Mediterranean work, *Tapiola.* Both first and second symphonies breathe the air of romanticism and although the formal concentration and strength of the mature Sibelius is to be discerned they belong to the period of his creative career that can for the sake of convenience be called nationalist-romantic.

In 1903 he wrote the *Violin Concerto,* but was as self-critical as he had been in the case of *En Saga* and the *Lemminkäinen Suite* and rewrote it. It was given in its final form in 1905 in Berlin with Richard Strauss conducting. In the winter of 1903–4 Sibelius went through a period of questioning and self-doubt; the results of this were two-fold: first, he decided to leave Helsinki and live in the country, and secondly, from the artistic point of view came a quite radical change of style of which the first results are to be seen in the third symphony. Sibelius's country house was at Järvenpää, about twenty-five miles north-east of Helsinki. It was to be Sibelius's home for the rest of his life. He named it Ainola after his wife. And there in 1904 he began the new symphony.

If the 1890s had seen Sibelius's reputation established among his countrymen and to a more limited extent in the neighbouring Scandinavian countries, the first decade of the present century was to see his struggle for international recognition begin in earnest. In 1905 he went to Berlin at Busoni's behest to conduct the second symphony; Hans Richter conducted the same work at a Hallé concert the same year in Manchester. In England Bantock, Henry Wood and others were championing his scores while critics like Ernest Newman and Rosa Newmarch took up their pens on his behalf. Indeed it was in London that the premiere of the *Symphony No. 3* was promised in 1907, though the work was not ready in time. (In fact it was given under Sibelius's own direction in Helsinki and then St Petersburg later that year.) But if the third symphony saw him moving in the direction of a neo-classicism and other works of the same period, *Nightride and Sunrise* and *Pohjola's Daughter* show him moving away from the overt romanticism of the first two symphonies, it was not until the fourth symphony that the movement towards austerity reached its climax. It was in 1908 that he came to London to conduct the third symphony and it was at this time that he became increasingly troubled by pains in the throat. This was ultimately diagnosed as a malignant growth and Sibelius underwent a number of operations for this. Coming as it did at the height of his career, threatening to cut his life short, this experience must have been traumatic and its effect on his art was no less far-reaching. He felt alienated from the current musical trends of the day, though he kept fully abreast of them. While he was working on his only mature quartet, *Voces Intimae,* written in Paris and London, he heard Debussy's *Nocturnes*, Elgar's first symphony, Bantock's *Omar Khayam* and met Bax, Goossens, d'Indy and Debussy himself.

Just after the first performance of the third symphony in 1907, Mahler visited Helsinki and the two composers met. Their oft-quoted exchange on the nature of the symphony reveals the difference of emphasis in their approach to the form. Sibelius said he admired 'its severity and style, and the profound logic that created an inner connection between all the motifs' to which Mahler replied: 'no, for me the symphony must be like the world. It must embrace everything'.

In the spring of 1910 Sibelius began his fourth symphony, his most remarkable, austere and concentrated work. The symphony matured slowly; Sibelius took it with him on various tours and eventually it was performed in April 1911 in Helsinki. Other recent works were included in the same programme, among them *Nightride and Sunrise* and *In Memoriam*; but the *Symphony No. 4* completely bewildered the audience and critics, being written in a very different style from anything Sibelius had composed before. It was one of the slowest of his works to gain recognition, but is now regarded by many as perhaps his masterpiece. In Sweden it had been received with boos, and in America it was abused as 'ultra-modern, dissonant and doleful'.

But the fourth symphony was not the only new work to

strike the deeper, more inward layers of feeling: *The Bard*, a short tone-poem of great tranquillity yet power, and the strange and mysterious *Luonnotar* for soprano and orchestra belong to this period of introspection. All these new works appear to break new ground in some way as does *The Oceanides,* written for the trip he was invited to make to America in 1914. Sibelius's reputation was by now well established; in 1912 he was offered a professorship at the Vienna Imperial Music Academy, and when he arrived in America he found himself far more famous than he had imagined.

Sibelius returned to Finland in July 1914, less than a month before the outbreak of the First World War. During the war financial difficulties increased as he was suddenly cut off from his royalties in Germany, and eventually he began his association with the Danish firm of Hansen. He also wrote a number of songs and small piano pieces, some for frankly commercial reasons, but he did begin work on his fifth symphony and finished it in time for his fiftieth birthday in 1915. This was treated almost as a national holiday in Finland, and Sibelius conducted the first performance of his *Symphony No. 5* on the day itself. But he was not entirely satisfied with the work and revised it twice, in 1916 and 1919, and reduced the number of movements from four to three. Though there was no actual fighting in Finland during the early part of the war, Sibelius felt his isolation from the rest of the world very keenly and in particular regretted the lack of contact with first-class foreign orchestras.

Save for the work on the fifth symphony, and the masterly *Humoresques* for violin and orchestra, the war years were pretty barren. Indeed during the civil war that broke out after the declaration of independence in 1917, Sibelius was subjected (like most of his countrymen) to genuine hardship and was forced to flee from Järvenpää and take refuge with his brother.

One of the remarkable things about Sibelius's symphonies is that it is difficult from the vantage point of one to predict the character of the next. After so austere and uncompromising a work as the fourth, who would have suspected so heroic a work as the fifth? And given the optimism of the fifth (1919) who would have foreseen a work like the sixth, whose language is as purified and free from rhetoric as it would be possible to imagine? And in terms of formal originality, the seventh symphony (1924) has few precedents in Sibelius's earlier output. In 1920 Sibelius was offered a chair at the newly-founded Eastman School of Music in the United States, but eventually decided against it. Although there was little evidence of it at the time, for Sibelius was highly active, his creative flame was beginning to burn out. After the seventh symphony only two major works were to come: the incidental music for a lavish Copenhagen production of Shakespeare's *Tempest* planned for the spring of 1926, and the symphonic poem, *Tapiola,* commissioned by Walter Damrosch for New York where it was first given the same year. Its terrifying evocation of the power of nature represented the end of the road, creatively speaking, for Sibelius. There were smaller pieces written during the late twenties, but nothing of real note. Later on he revised some earlier works, including two of the *Lemminkäinen* legends.

In the early thirties there were rumours that he had completed an eighth symphony, and the Sibelius Society, founded in London by HMV in June 1932, proposed to include the new symphony among its recordings. It would seem that an eighth symphony either existed in an incomplete form during the thirties or was completed and subject to constant revision before being destroyed. Always highly self-critical, Sibelius was particularly conscious of the searchlight that was directed on this new symphony; it was promised to Koussevitzky and to Beecham among others. One story has it that the score was delivered to a copyist who was woken in the middle of the night and asked to return it. In 1945, Sibelius told Basil Cameron that the eighth symphony had been written 'many times' but that he was not happy with it.

During the thirties Sibelius's reputation reached its height in the Anglo-Saxon world. Moreover his work satisfied the public appetite for new orchestral repertoire at a time when modern music was either inaccessible in idiom or musically insubstantial. Cecil Gray made enormous claims for the symphonies and Constant Lambert in his brilliant *Music Ho!* added his voice to the many others raised on Sibelius's behalf. This in itself may well have had an inhibiting effect on the composer, always self-critical and now almost a recluse, fearful that a symphony that did not meet the expectations of his admirers would damage the reputation he had built up. If the wilder claims made on Sibelius's behalf ensured a reaction in the sixties in England and America, the fact that his work enjoyed wide currency in Germany during the Nazi period served to prejudice many German and Continental critics against it in the immediate post-war years. He lived in retirement in Järvenpää, revered and honoured almost as much as a great statesman, until his death from a cerebral haemorrhage in September 1957.

Sibelius's influence and fame were enormous until the fifties when the inevitable reaction began to set in. The younger generation then came to feel that in spite of his great originality (few composers are so immediately recognizable as he is) he was a composer who looked backwards rather than forwards, though this is not to deny his genius in giving new life to symphonic form. The austerity and restraint of many of his works, like the fourth and sixth symphonies, are a welcome counterbalance to the excesses of post-romanticism.

Though Sibelius was a nationalist in one sense (though perhaps it would be more accurate to describe him as regional rather than nationalist) he did not draw on Finnish folk music for his inspiration. True, the intonation of Finnish speech undoubtedly affected his melodic thinking and he did make a study of Karelian folk music at one time, but he made no overt use of folk material. Nor did the most important of his contemporaries, Yrjö Kilpinen (1892–1959) who, incidentally, delivered his funeral oration. Although Sibelius wrote about a hundred songs, mostly settings of Swedish poetry, though there are a handful of songs in Finnish, these are overshadowed by the symphonies and symphonic poems. Kilpinen's reputation on the other hand rests almost exclusively on his prolific output of songs; indeed he left little other than Lieder though there are six piano sonatas and other pieces. Kilpinen's art is sadly underrated nowadays though his songs are often highly personal and concentrated.

The only other Scandinavian symphonist of international stature is Carl Nielsen, who was born in the same year as Sibelius, 1865, in a small village on the island of Funen, Denmark, not far from Odense, the birthplace of Hans Christian Andersen. His art forms a highly interesting contrast with that of Sibelius,[1] as does his career. He was born of humble, sturdy origins; his father was a house painter and village musician and the family numbered no fewer than twelve children. Although the family was poor, it was musical and Nielsen's talent was not discouraged. He learned the violin and then the trumpet, joining the local battalion when he was fourteen as a regimental musician. At Odense he was able to see how an orchestra worked and also met an ageing pianist who introduced him to the work of Haydn, Mozart, Beethoven and later on Bach.

His first efforts at composition had been in the days when he played in the village band and had tried his hand at writing dance tunes. In his teens he began, like Sibelius, writing chamber music mostly modelled on the Viennese classics, and in 1883 went to Copenhagen in the hope of gaining admission to the Conservatoire. Gade, still its head, examined a quartet he showed him and agreed to accept him, provided he could pass an audition as a violinist. He studied at the Conservatoire for two years (1884–86) and like Sibelius became a proficient violinist but not a very good pianist. Although this proved inhibiting for Sibelius, whose piano writing reveals his lack of sympathy with the instrument, Nielsen composed a quantity of highly original piano music later in life, including the *Suite* Opus 45 written for Schnabel. His early music, the G major *String Quintet* and the first two quartets show the influence of Johan Svendsen and Dvořák, but his breakthrough came with the *Suite for Strings* Opus 1, which was given at the Tivoli Gardens with great public success. Svendsen was the conductor at the premiere of Nielsen's *Symphony No. 1* in 1894, a work of astonishing melodic vitality and freshness. Although the influence of Brahms is to be found, Nielsen's distinctively individual voice is already apparent. The chromaticism of the slow movement is free from the claustrophobic atmosphere one encounters in Franck, whom Nielsen incidentally admired, and the texture remains spacious and open. Even as early as the first symphony, Nielsen's concept of 'progressive tonality' is present; the work begins in G minor and ends in C, and tonal conflict remains the central theme in his symphonic thinking. Nielsen took part in the first performance of this symphony, stepping forward from his place in the second violins to acknowledge the applause. He served as a member of the Royal Orchestra for some fourteen years and his duties there may well have served to diminish the quantity of his output.

Nielsen's next symphony, *The Four Temperaments*, has the spontaneity of its predecessor but is more compact in its argument and more tautly constructed. The debt to Brahms is still discernible (the second group of the first movement is an obvious instance) but there is great freshness of invention and an abundance of vitality. But these years saw not only the two symphonies and some delightful choral works like *Hymnus Amoris* and *Søvnen* (*Sleep*) but the four quartets and two operas. The quartets show an increasing mastery and independence of style; the fourth (1906) not only forges a language entirely his own but remains probably the finest Scandinavian string quartet with the possible exception of *Voces intimae*. After 1906 Nielsen never returned to the quartet; indeed apart from the *Wind Quintet* he showed little interest in chamber music. Nor did he attempt another opera after this date; *Saul and David* (1900–2) and *Maskarade* (1906) were his only operatic ventures though he toyed with plans for another opera, albeit half-heartedly, later in life. His genius was basically no more operatic in outlook than was Sibelius's, though his achievement in this field was, of course, the greater. *Saul and David* has some noble music; indeed its musical strength is greater than its dramatic power. *Maskarade,* Nielsen's comic opera, is a delightful and sparkling score and the nearest Scandinavia has come to an operatic masterpiece. In 1909 Nielsen succeeded Svendsen as conductor of the Royal Orchestra and held this post for some six years; he also conducted the Gothenburg Orchestra for a time. From the pre-war years come the *Sinfonia Espansiva* (1911) and the *Violin Concerto* (1912) which show him deepening his art, the symphony in particular showing a greater command over his musical material and an ability to think in longer musical paragraphs. But the 1914–18 war, although it did not directly involve Denmark, came as a tremendous psychic shock; the spectacle of unremitting slaughter, senseless destruction and suffering haunted his imagination. His music assumes an added dimension; its contours are harder, its harmonies less rich, its lines darker and with its greater complexity came greater depth. The *Symphony No. 4* (1916), the *Suite for Piano* Opus 45, and the *Symphony No. 5* (1922) all reveal a profound imagination disturbed by the terrible events of the war, yet still fundamentally convinced, as we know from the programme of the fourth symphony (*L'Inestinguibile*), that life would triumph.

The explosive power of this symphony and its more complex tonal structure are taken a stage further in the fifth, whose opening is among his most inspired pages. It is interesting to see the way in which Sibelius's and Nielsen's paths differ during the immediate post-war period. Sibelius turned away from the iconoclasm of the twenties, turned inwards on himself; works like the *Symphony No. 6* (1923) and *Tapiola* (1926) are a record of an inner experience wholly unrelated to the art of the period: hence they have a quality that never dates. Their sense of communion with nature and awe of natural forces takes pride of place over human relationships. Nielsen's art seems more deeply affected by the breakdown of values that marks the period and disturbed by the disintegration of musical language; the wider vision and greater depth his music acquires after, say, the fourth symphony testify to the spiritual growth he underwent. And just as the fifth and seventh symphonies of Sibelius are unique formally, so Nielsen's fifth charts new ground. The *Clarinet Concerto* almost seems as if it is music from another planet; it is surely worlds removed from the Nielsen of the second symphony. Yet the complexities of the fifth symphony and the concerto, the three late piano pieces or *Commotio* go hand in hand with a simple, diatonic art. Nielsen never lost sight of his folk origins; *Springtime on Fünen,* a work of disarmingly touching inspiration, is as simple structurally as the two-movement edifice of the fifth symphony is complex. Likewise the simplicity of the *Piano Pieces for Young and Old* that come from 1930, only a year before his death, is in striking contrast with a work like *Commotio* for organ, composed at about the same time. Nielsen's reputation was slower to penetrate outside the Scandinavian countries than Sibelius's though there had been performances of his works; he conducted the fourth symphony in London in the twenties and Furtwängler had conducted the fifth in Germany, but the vogue for his work was essentially a post-Second World War phenomenon. When he died Nielsen's art seemed to be on the threshold of new discoveries; his music developed a toughness and independence comparable only with Sibelius's though very different from it. The achievement of both masters is twofold: to show, first, that within the discipline and concentration of the symphony there was still a great deal that could be accomplished, and second, that Scandinavia was no longer a backward outpost on the periphery of Europe. They achieved for Scandinavia in the first quarter of the century what Ibsen and Strindberg had achieved for Scandinavian literature before them.

10 Scandinavian composers since Sibelius

It is natural that such outsize musical personalities as Sibelius and Nielsen should have dominated their age; their achievements are comparable only with those of the great Scandinavian dramatists of the last century. Yet if they have overshadowed their contemporaries, their achievement has served to stimulate a host of other composers, less in stature perhaps but nonetheless interesting. Indeed it is true to say that the Scandinavian countries between them have made a contribution out of all proportion to their size. Each of them has an independent musical tradition that differs in important respects from its neighbours even though certain parallels can be discerned.

National sentiment and circumstances play their part in the development of any composer or group of composers: the Swedes, though the most reluctant to relinquish the traditional nationalism that coloured their expressive vocabulary at the beginning of the century, have in the last two or three decades been the quickest to respond to Continental influence. By contrast Norway is perhaps one of the least outward-looking of musical cultures: it has pursued a different course, content to cultivate a folk-tradition that dominated its musical speech until relatively late; only the isolated figure of Fartein Valen tilled a solitary furrow against this background. In Finland Sibelius's powerful symphonic art cast so formidable a shadow that his immediate successors found his influence more impressive than inspiring and the sunless forests of *Tapiola* have swallowed up all but a few of his imitators. Yet in Kilpinen Finland has produced a song composer of the greatest mastery whose stature far outstrips his meagre representation in the current repertoire. In Denmark the influence of Nielsen seems to have had a less inhibiting effect on younger Danish composers than did Sibelius on the younger Finns. But the fact remains that few Scandinavian composers have succeeded in establishing themselves in the international repertoire even though some of them have enjoyed a short-lived vogue in various circles. Hence this survey, rather than relating a list of little-known names to their national background, will be strictly selective and makes no apology on this count. Those requiring an account on national lines are referred to the many admirable surveys that already exist.

Few of their younger contemporaries failed to respond in some way to either Sibelius or Nielsen. The Norwegians were perhaps the exception; Sibelius at least exerted little or no influence on the Norwegian musical scene. Grieg's art still dominated the imagination of most Norwegians; indeed it had even served to fertilize the young Sibelius as late as the 1890s, just as Nielsen's stylistic outlook (and his orchestration) owes something to his contact with the Norwegian, Svendsen. Sweden was a different matter; both stylistic poles exerted their magnetism over composers as far removed in time as Stenhammar and Blomdahl.

Wilhelm Stenhammar (1871–1927) possessed a quiet, aristocratic cast of mind and has never made much headway outside his own country. True, there is a certain pallor about some of his weaker music and his debt to Brahms and at times even Reger seems a handicap. Yet at his best there is real character and individuality, and his personality, though not immediately assertive, becomes more sympathetic and compelling with familiarity. This quiet-spoken composer has perhaps something of Fauré's gentleness and Elgar's ambience though in idiom he resembles neither. One of his finest works is the *Serenade for Orchestra* Opus 31 (1913 rev. 1919); possibly his masterpiece, it has great charm and subtlety of colouring. If it lacks the robust melodic vitality that ensures immediate popularity it nonetheless has a genuine vein of poetry and fantasy. The fourth movement, the *Romance*, is a beautifully-wrought piece, full of nostalgia and delicacy; the intensity of its feeling for the evanescent, a quality it shares with Elgar, and a gentle melancholy are its most distinctive features. But the *Serenade* has an exuberance of invention and a lightness of touch in its handling of the orchestra that place Stenhammar well above his contemporaries. In his *Symphony No. 2* (1915) Stenhammar offers further evidence of qualities of mind and sensibility that make him worthy of wider attention. His command of the symphonic process and his technical resources are more complete than any of his Scandinavian contemporaries, save Sibelius and Nielsen, while the finest of the six string quartets and some of the songs bear witness to his fastidious craftsmanship and cultivated taste. His music has a quality of reserve that masks an underlying warmth and though there are times when his sense of structure is vulnerable (the close of the *String Quartet No. 3*, 1897–1900) his voice is a distinctive one and its accents far more personal than at first appears.

Stenhammar was not content merely to cultivate a provincial nationalism for his sympathies were primarily classical. He was a formidable pianist, as one would deduce from his two piano concertos, though he wrote surprisingly little for the keyboard; he was a fine Beethoven interpreter and as a conductor championed the cause of Sibelius and Nielsen. He was, incidentally, the dedicatee of Sibelius's sixth symphony.

Hugh Alfvén (1872–1960), Ture Rangström (1884–1947) and Kurt Atterberg (b. 1887) are less subtle and complex; Alfvén's art is the most overtly national and he seems to have looked to neither of the two great Nordic symphonists for inspiration but rather to Svendsen and Sinding. His *Midsommarvaka* (*Midsummer Watch*) is in a sense the Swedish equivalent of Svendsen's *Norwegian Rhapsodies*, a brilliantly effective repertoire piece that deserves its wide popularity. In the symphonic canvas neither he nor Rangström was fully at ease, though Alfvén's technique was the more fully developed to meet the symphonic challenge. Rangström was self-taught and it is in his songs that his talent appears at its strongest: he was a genuine lyricist and at his best, in his Bo Bergman settings or in the *Bön till natten* (*Prayer to the night*) he achieves a simplicity and purity of style that are affecting. Atterberg, the most prolific symphonist of this generation and the one who gained the widest international recognition, is more impressive in simpler, lyrical vein as in the *Suite* for violin, viola and string orchestra (1919).

In Finland few composers of this generation escaped the fate of being overshadowed by their great countryman. Leevi Madetoja (1887–1947) did win a hearing outside Finland but the Sibelian tutelage, to judge from his *Symphony No. 2*, weighed heavily on him. Only Kilpinen seems to have escaped; his is a limited but nonetheless impressive achievement. His devotion to Lieder is as complete as, say, that of Medtner to the piano and his output consists of some seven hundred songs and a small quantity of instrumental music. Despite the debt to Wolf and the German tradition, the neglect of his art seems unaccountable. There is a dark, brooding fantasy that pervades the best of his work; the psychological insight and intensity of his settings of Morgenstern's *Lieder um den Tod* or a song like *Mondschein* show that he shares with Sibelius the ability to gain the maximum musical effect with minimum expressive means. The comparison made with the Swiss, Othmar Schoeck, is telling; both artists possess searching qualities of imagination, an ability to distill atmosphere and a formidable technical equipment. Both are underrated outside their own countries. Where Kilpinen scores over a composer like Rangström, say, is in his economy of means: he can suggest far more complex moods by means of a simple stroke and create far richer resonances. Where Rangström scores is in the freshness and at times naïve quality of his inspiration which serves to make his art so direct in appeal.

In a sense Sweden was freer than her neighbours and more readily able to draw on their great figures: she had no Grieg, Sibelius or Nielsen towering in the foreground. Hence she produced few 'outsiders' like the Dane, Rued Langgaard (1893–1952), the Finn, Aarre Merikanto (1893–1958) and the Norwegian, Fartein Valen (1887–1952). Valen is in fact the most straightforward of the three, a kind of Norwegian Skalkottas, sharing with the Greek composer a strong sense of atmosphere. Like the other two he suffered considerable neglect and his music made practically no headway outside Norway until after the Second World War, when he enjoyed a shortlived vogue in both his own country and in England. He was born in Stavanger but spent his childhood years in Madagascar, returning to Norway for his studies. After reading philology at the University of Oslo, he threw up his career and decided to devote himself entirely to music, studying in Berlin under Max Bruch. After the First World War, in the early twenties, he went to Italy and spent a good deal of time there before finally settling in 1939 in the Norwegian village of Valevåg, where he remained until his death. His early music seems to have donned a Brahmsian-Regerish habit, and his disaffection with the traditional expressive vocabulary emerges in the *Piano Trio* (1924) on which he had laboured for more than seven years and which marks a watershed in his creative career. It is the absence of a tonal centre rather than the application of strictly serial techniques that lies at the heart of his style. He has written a quantity of descriptive music, most of it exquisitely scored, and revealing an imagination of considerable power. *Le cimetière marin* and *La isla de las calmas* (1934) show an individual sensibility at work.

The *Violin Concerto* (1940) shows a delicacy of feeling and a poetry that makes one regret all the more its deficient rhythmic vitality. Like the Berg concerto, which Valen is said not to have known at the time, the work ends with a chorale, *Jesu meine Zuversicht* on to which various strands of the concerto are grafted. Valen was by nature a recluse and his music is that of a spirit who chooses isolation quite deliberately. His symphonies fall outside the Scandinavian tradition and his often poignant harmonic language seems to make little contact with that of any other Norwegian artist. If Valen had some of the insights of a visionary so had Rued Langgaard whose music is currently being rediscovered. Like Havergal Brian in this country his music is difficult to assess because of its inaccessibility; nor is it always easy to judge what springs from an innate originality and what comes from the kind of originality acquired and engendered by neglect. He was strongly religious by temperament and something of a visionary; his works bear titles like *The Defiance of Heaven* (his sixth symphony) or *Music of the Spheres.* His output is large and includes no fewer than sixteen symphonies and a church opera, *Kremasco*, most of it written in total isolation. He was not an admirer of Nielsen in his maturity though his melodic lines do not always escape his influence; indeed he was almost alone in Denmark in admiring the late romantics, Liszt, Schumann and Gade as models. And yet his work, alongside passages of commonplace utterance, has moments of a wild-eyed visionary quality. *Music of the Spheres* employs tone-clusters, a piano played directly on the strings and other forward-looking devices. If he lacks the breadth of a symphonist (judging from the few of his symphonies I have been able to hear) he has an undoubted independence that reminds one of Ives.

The Finnish composer, Aarre Merikanto is an exact contemporary of Langgaard's, though he died somewhat later and likewise suffered cruel neglect. His models were Reger, with whom he studied for a short time, and Scriabin, and his opera *Juha* (1922) is said to bear a striking resemblance in its relationship between speech and melody with Janáček's *Katya Kabanova,* though the scoring owes something to Strauss. Like Langgaard, Merikanto was an 'outsider' and his eclecticism served to bewilder his comtemporaries rather than stimulate them. He was prolific: three piano concertos, four violin concertos and two cello concertos as well as tone poems. Acclaim eventually came late in life but too late to secure him any measure of recognition outside his own country.

Harald Saeverud (b.1897) has the most distinctive profile and the most completely formed personality of all modern Norwegian composers. His melodic style is diatonic, aphoristic and direct; his harmonies are uncomplicated but spiced by the clash of independent lines while his sense of rhythm is uncommonly robust. He spent his formative years along the Norwegian seaboard and studied in Bergen with Borghild Holmsen; the Westlandsmusik, the folk music of that part of the country, played a decisive role in his musical development. He is, as the charming keyboard miniatures he has written show, a master of the musical epigram, in which wit and elegance come into their own. Their simplicity never seems arch, and though they are sometimes only two-part they are fashioned with enormous care and artistry. These *Slåtter og stev fra Siljustøl* and the sonatinas for piano are quite unlike anything else in contemporary music. Saeverud has never consciously modelled his style on folk music but he has, to use his own words, tried to absorb its spirit 'just as to keep fit and healthy one eats fine Norwegian food'. To many outsiders he seems more truly Norwegian than any of his contemporaries. Indeed Robert Simpson called him 'as Norwegian as Sibelius is Finnish, and in a similar sense. The best of his music seems to express the spirit of his country's past, strange, mysterious, vigorous, the harshness and drama of its scenery and its intemperate climate. This music is not concerned with polite conversation; roughness is frequent and a tough core of hard-headed obstinacy may be felt. Yet he is a sensitive, civilized composer with a rich and salty sense of humour that often warms his asperities.'[1] His output now includes nine symphonies, the most recent dating from 1966, of which three composed during the Second World War – the fifth (*Quasi una fantasia,* 1941), the sixth (*Sinfonia Dolorosa,* 1942) and the seventh (*Salme-Symfoni,* 1944–45) – show him at his most vital. In fact the war years saw a veritable upsurge of creative energy, some of it like the *Kjempevise-slåtten* highly combative in character. The latter became something of a symbol of resistance during the war and its two companions, *Galdreslåtten* and *Siljuslåtten*, both dating from 1943, share its rhythmic drive and seemingly limitless energy.

His *Piano Concerto* (1949) is a well-wrought piece, terse in utterance and positive in feeling, and his incidental music for Ibsen's *Peer Gynt* (1947) brought him widespread recognition beyond Norway for its inventiveness and originality. The short-breathed quality of his thinking disqualifies the symphonies from being completely successful; the monothematic sixth, written in memory of a friend killed by the Germans, is extremely powerful but less convincing structurally. The seventh is highly impressive, its sonorities haunting and its atmosphere wholly individual. Its failings, like those of its predecessor, are structural and such is its strength that they seem of little account. His lyric gift and his dry, laconic yet kindly wit have gone to produce a figure unique in twentieth-century Scandinavia and in terms of sheer personality he outstrips almost all of his countrymen.

To a non-specialist the Norwegian folk-tradition seems stronger and more highly characterized than those of the other Scandinavian countries; hence its stronger hold over the imagination of Norwegian composers. Of course there are exceptions of which Fartein Valen is the best known, but there are others, like Pauline Hall (1890–1969), who have opened the windows on the outside world. Her sympathies were primarily Gallic and her music is as urbane and civilized as that of any Frenchman. Even as conservative a figure as David Monrad-Johansen (b. 1886), Grieg's first biographer, succumbed to the French for a time. But generally speaking Norway was slower to respond to the cosmopolitan spirit than was Sweden, and the attraction of folk- or folk-inspired material persisted longer than possibly anywhere else. Ludvig Irgens Jensen (1894–1969) is certainly at his best in a folk-inspired context: the bigger orchestral pieces, even the work with which he made his initial breakthrough, the *Passacaglia for Orchestra,* seem ill-suited to his particular lyrical talents. Just how good these are, I think, can be seen not only from the best of his songs, but in a work like the *Partita Sinfonica* (1937), based on music for the dramatic poem *Driftkaren* by the Norwegian poet Kinck. This has great freshness and lyrical spontaneity though the influence of early Nielsen is evident in its harmonic flavouring. Eivind Groven (b. 1901) and Sparre Olsen (b. 1903) are fairly and squarely centred in the folk-tradition too. Like Jensen's, Groven's talent is primarily seen at its finest in smaller forms.

The Norwegian composer of this generation who has received more international attention than almost any other except Saeverud and Valen is Klaus Egge (b. 1906), who is clearly attracted to the bigger forms and has four symphonies to his credit. Egge studied for a time with Fartein Valen and his work shows evidence of distinguished craftsmanship and seriousness of purpose. The musical ideas themselves are less characterful and compelling; the first symphony for all its breadth suffers from this deficiency of melodic invention and the most impressive of his works is probably the *Violin Concerto,* in which inspiration and craftsmanship seem more evenly matched. Folk-inspired material plays relatively little part in his mature work, though the early music did reflect its influence. His language is diatonic, his textures often polyphonic and effectively scored and his music has the stamp of integrity. But it lacks the freshness, character and spontaneity of Saeverud. Folk music plays a major role in the prodigious activity of Geirr Tveitt (b. 1908) whose output includes three operas, two one-act operas, five piano concertos and some thirty piano sonatas. He has been an energetic collector of folk music and has published over a hundred folk-tunes in highly effective orchestral arrangements.

In the absence of a commanding national figure like Grieg, the Swedish situation was different. Swedish composers were the most outward-looking and their reaction against their post-nationalist elders like Alfvén, Rangström and Atterberg was far more immediate. The most commanding figure of this generation is without doubt that of Hilding Rosenberg (b. 1892), a contemporary of Honegger and Milhaud, of Kilpinen in Finland and Laszlo Lajtha in Hungary. He has in fact been compared with the Swiss master, Frank Martin (b. 1890) and though there is no resemblance in terms of idiom, they share a taste for pale textures and both have a certain Old Testament dignity. Martin however only came into his own relatively late in his career and certain recognizable features of speech at times approach the obsessive. Rosenberg's sense of atmosphere is less strong perhaps, but the emotional spectrum is a good deal wider; Martin's muted colouring witnesses a fastidious palette but his thinking is not primarily that of a symphonist, whereas Rosenberg, whatever his failings, is genuinely concerned with the symphonic process. The comparison is thus not a fruitful one but it does serve the purpose of placing Rosenberg in some kind of European context. He was born in Bosjökloster in southern Sweden and his first works, including a symphony, not unnaturally reflected the influence of Sibelius; few Swedish composers escaped it and Sibelian habits of mind persist in Rosenberg's work as late as the thirties. But his was a searching, outward-looking mind; the Schoenberg of the *Kammersymphonie No. 1* exercised his fascination over him in the first of his quartets (1920), while during the mid-fifties he returned to serial methods of organization in the six string quartets (nos. 7–12) that he wrote at the behest of the Swedish Radio. He is not only a prolific composer but works with enthusiasm and at high speed; the six quartets in question occupied him for not much longer than a year (1956–57). Like many other Swedish composers of the day (Nystroem was another) he spent some time in Paris and a score like *Orfeus i stan* (*Orpheus in Town*) shows that the sophistication of *Les Six* had not been lost on him. Bo Wallner notices Milhaud's influence as early as the second quartet (1923) while both Honegger and Hindemith exercised a strong fascination for him. Yet if his style reflects a diversity of sympathies his personality is nonetheless a distinct one. The second symphony (*Sinfonia grave,* 1928–36) is a watershed in his career and with it he establishes his symphonic credentials without any manner of doubt. It has the breadth of the symphonist with long sweeping lines and a genuine sense of momentum. Its slow movement has a real poetic eloquence; though the idiom is unmistakeably Nordic, its vision seems broader. Only in terms of sheer concentration does this fall short of the symphonic ideal. Rosenberg was also enormously prolific in other forms; the opera *Resa till Amerika* (*Journey to America*), with its folkloristic intermezzi, dates from this period (1932). And so does the opera, *Marionetter* (1939) whose overture shows his style at its most cosmopolitan. Rosenberg was for a few years at the helm of the Opera Orchestra and his interest in opera has been lifelong.

The war years in a sense were his most productive. The *Symphony No. 3* (1939) drew on literary inspiration (Romain Rolland's *Jean Christophe*) and originally bore the subtitle *The Four Ages of Man.* Indeed it was first performed with intervening narration, but Rosenberg subsequently withdrew its title and made some revisions including the excision of the fugal section in the scherzo. The opening idea has an angularity that suggests Honegger or Hindemith and, like some of Martin's ideas, makes use of all the twelve notes of the chromatic scale but arranges them in such a way as to exploit their tonal implications. The first movement generates writing of great expressive power and to my mind the second group is one of his most delicately-imagined inspirations. The muted colourings and transparent scoring clothe invention of singular poetry; the whole paragraph breathes the air of gentle melancholy so characteristic of the Swedish sensibility. The ruminative second movement is full of memorably poetic ideas and the symphony is probably the finest that was produced in Sweden between the wars. Both its successors are choral: the fourth symphony (*St Johannes Uppenbarelse* or *The Revelation of St John the Divine*, 1940) and the fifth (*Örtragårdsmästaren* or *Hortulanus*, 1944) though the latter is on a smaller scale and scored for smaller forces. *The Revelation of St John* is a powerfully sustained and highly effective work reflecting something of the same neo-classical outlook as Hindemith's and having something of Walton's dramatic flair. The *Symphony No. 5* is an underrated piece, too; it is simple and direct in utterance and in many of its textures one notices affinities with Carl Nielsen. Much of its invention is modal and in mood it often attains a serene tranquillity. It is one of the least played of his works and one of the most rewarding. Another large-scale work is the opera-oratorio based on Mann's trilogy, *Joseph and his Brethren*, perhaps the most ambitious and certainly one of the most impressive of all his works. Indeed it has some of the most imaginative music he has penned.

Rosenberg's catalogue of works is long and his output, particularly in the post-war years, is by no means even. He sets great store (and rightly) by his quality of craftsmanship and yet there are times when his sheer facility creates problems. Some of his music lacks concentration and density of incident; the *Cello Concerto No. 2* is a case in point. The lyrical expressiveness that Wallner speaks of in his post-war period 'taking the form of long surging melodic lines' often degenerates into an aimlessness and a deficiency of creative spontaneity. Not even as fine a work as the purely instrumental *Symphony No. 6* (1951) exhibits a uniform sense of purpose though its breadth and imaginative detail are rewarding. The *Concerto for string orchestra* (1946) on the other hand shows him at his most concentrated, without any loss of spontaneity. Of the twelve quartets, the fourth (1939) has been overshadowed by the much admired sixth (1953), which is a pity since it has both character and a strong sense of purpose.

Rosenberg's achievement was not merely to open the doors to cosmopolitan thinking but to do so without any loss of identity. Though international in sympathies he remained recognizably Swedish and his sensibility was enriched as a result. His role as a teacher has been an important one and his pupils number many of the most influential figures of the next generation. His immediate contemporary, Gösta Nystroem (1890–1966) is hardly nowadays heard outside Sweden but he had both a distinct personality and a genuine talent. His sympathies were primarily Gallic (he lived for most of the twenties in Paris where he studied painting) and Honegger was a dominant influence in his music. Among the finest of his works is the *Sinfonia espressiva,* a powerfully conceived and cogently argued piece that occupied him during the first half of the thirties. His incidental music to *The Merchant of Venice,* some of the songs and in particular the *Sånger vid havet* as well as the *Sinfonia Concertante* for cello and orchestra (1944) bear witness to a genuine lyrical impulse though the post-war years found him less compelling. The much-admired *Sinfonia del mare* shows him in discursive mood and his thematic invention is a good deal less distinctive than its reputation would lead one to expect. Nystroem, like Stenhammar, lived on the western seaboard and once spoke of himself as 'a worshipper of absolute music' though at the same time confessing that he was an 'incurable romantic'.

The next generation of Swedish composers nearly all echo the first of those sentiments: indeed neo-classic ideals served to inspire neighbouring Scandinavian composers Klaus

Egge in Norway and Herman Koppel, Niels Viggo Bentzon and Vagn Holmboe in Denmark. By far the best known is Dag Wirén (b. 1905) whose masterly *Serenade for Strings* (1938) has won a firm place in the international repertoire. In a sense Simpson was right, I think, to view him as 'the most natural talent in twentieth-century Swedish music even if his achievement is not as substantial as, say, Rosenberg's'. Wirén's generation also includes Lars-Erik Larsson (b. 1908), Gunnar de Frumerie (b. 1908) and Erland von Koch (b. 1910) all of whom are neo-classic in outlook and have high standards of craftsmanship. Wirén and de Frumerie both studied in Paris while Larsson went to Vienna and became for a while a student of Berg. Wirén has the freshest and most highly characterized melodic style; his invention is sunny and genial for the most part though in more reflective vein he distills an atmosphere more intense than any of his immediate contemporaries. With the most economical of means he can portray more vividly a poetic image that is both memorable and distinctively Swedish. His tendency to think in too short a span inhibits his symphonic writing; his ideas in, for example, the slow movement of the *Cello Concerto* are not given room in which to expand. He arrives at a climax which he fails to sustain long enough to satisfy the expectations aroused in the listener. Even the imaginative *Symphony No. 4* (1952) is flawed in this way though the work is full of fantasy. But Wirén is less at ease in the symphony than he is smaller forms; his recourse to monothematicism in the fourth symphony, as a means of engendering unity, shows his awareness of this. It is in the *Divertimento for Orchestra* and the famous *Serenade* that his musical equipment best matches his artistic ambitions and that the means harmonize with the ends. Both Nielsen and Sibelius were formative influences, his avowed musical credo being, 'I believe in God, Mozart and Carl Nielsen!' Though in the *Symphony No. 3* (1943–44) Sibelian figures of speech loom large, the fact remains that Wirén's personality shines through everything he does from his biggest works to his film music. He has contributed some highly atmospheric scores to Ingmar Bergman's comedies made in the mid-fifties. His chamber music is neglected outside Sweden (and even inside it); yet his *Quartet No. 4* (1952–53) is one of the finest chamber works in the literature of post-war Swedish music and, like most of Wirén's work, neither courts popular appeal nor takes refuge in obscurity but remains content to be its unpretentious self.

Larsson is rather more eclectic; whereas Dag Wirén's outlook is almost exclusively Nordic, Larsson has some of the cosmopolitan elements we have encountered in Rosenberg. True, the opening of *Förklädd Gud*, his oratorio based on Hjalmar Gullberg, is Nielsen pure and simple; so, too, is the slow movement of his fine *Saxophone Concerto*. But there are numerous works from the *Sinfonietta* onwards in which broader geographical tastes and sympathies are felt. Like Rosenberg, Larsson has not hesitated to move away from the conventional neo-classicism of his generation when this has suited his artistic book. He is a craftsman of the first order and more readily able to sustain a musical argument than is Dag Wirén. The slow movement of his *Music for Orchestra* (1950) shows a vein of introspection and poetry far removed from the extrovert feelings of the (justly popular) *Pastoral Suite*, an excellent companion-piece to the Wirén *Serenade*.

As a whole *Music for Orchestra* is more responsive to European influences than anything of Wirén's even though there is still no doubt as to its identity. Nonetheless there are elements that inhabit the Hindemithian lingua franca of the day.

These two strands, an attraction towards the central European tradition and an allegiance to the smaller-scale pastoral idiom of Wirén, persist throughout his career. The *Variations for Orchestra* (1962) illustrate the former and show him seeking an increasing complexity of means, while the twelve concertinos he wrote during the mid-fifties at the behest of the Swedish Radio show his continued skill at turning out lighter music. The *Violin Concerto* (1952) has a lush Waltonesque ambience and shows Larsson's lyrical powers at their most persuasive. It deserves (and one day no doubt will establish) a firm place in the international repertory. There is, too, a fine *Missa brevis.* Even if he does not present so highly defined a profile as does Wirén, Larsson has a generous musical personality. Gunnar de Frumerie, though a less assertive personality, is a fastidious craftsman who, like Koppel in Denmark, is content to work within established traditions. His music is civilized and polished and his chamber music and songs have genuine substance: his art is wholly unostentatious.

The Danish situation differs from that of the other Scandinavian countries. Copenhagen is in some ways the most northerly 'European' city rather than just another Scandinavian capital; it has the feel of a great metropolis. Nielsen's inheritance, for example, is part Scandinavian – Danish folk music, Svendsen – and part European – Brahms and Dvořák. His shadow in turn dominated the Danish musical scene between the two wars and few escaped it. Even the 'outsider', Rued Langgaard, was no exception. Knud Jeppessen, born in 1892, the same year as Rosenberg, was a Nielsen pupil and a scholar of international repute; he is the author of *The Style of Palestrina and the Dissonance.* His language is diatonic, his sense of line strong and his harmonies reflect his sympathy with Nielsen, whose influence is readily discernible, particularly in the songs. His most widely-known work is the *Te deum Danicum* but such of his music as I have seen has none of the dry accents of the scholar but springs from a real creative impulse.

Most of the composers of this generation, like Poul Schierbeck, Finn Høffding or Fleming Weis, have made relatively little headway outside Scandinavia, though Høffding's *Det er ganske vist* (*Once upon a time*, 1943) did gain some currency at one time. The best-known figure is Knudaage Riisager (b. 1897), an Estonian by birth who settled in Copenhagen at an early age and joined the Danish civil

30 Jean Sibelius (1865–1957), the great Finnish symphonist, in 1945.

31 Sibelius as a young man.

32 Carl Nielsen (1865–1931) was the first Danish composer of international importance, he evolved a pragmatic, angular and strikingly individual language.

33 Harald Saeverud (b. 1897), Norway's most distingusihed composer; his music owes much to traditional Norwegian scales, rhythms and polyphony.

34 Fartein Valen (1887–1952), a Norwegian composer who lived as a recluse and developed his own style of atonal polyphony.

35 Hilding Rosenberg (b. 1892), a leading Swedish composer and conductor.

36 Knudaage Riisager (b. 1897), a pupil of Roussel and in later life president of the Danish League of Composers.

37 Vagn Holmboe (b. 1909) is a major Danish composer who has assimilated folk influences into a highly evolved personal style.

38 Gösta Nystroem (1890–1966) photographed in 1966: a Swedish composer, critic and painter.

39 Niels Viggo Bentzon (b. 1919), a Danish composer and pianist, at the piano (1967).

40 Arne Nordheim (b. 1931) and his family; this Swedish composer has been much concerned with electronic music.

41 The Finnish composer Joonas Kokkonen (b. 1920) photographed in 1970.

service, ending up at the Ministry of Finance. He studied for a time with Peder Gram and then went to Paris where he became a Roussel pupil and studied for a while with Paul le Flem. Like Pauline Hall in Norway or Uuno Klami in Finland, Riisager's sympathies were primarily Gallic and he became an enthusiastic admirer of Stravinsky and *Les Six*. His reputation outside Denmark rests largely on his ballet scores and other lighter works, like the *Concertino for trumpet and strings*, in which his high spirits most readily find their outlet. *Slaraffenland* (*Fool's Paradise*) shows how effectively his streak of gaiety and exuberance can operate and a more searching score such as *Qarrtsiluni* shows his imagination stretching itself (though not wholly successfully) against a more challenging canvas.

One other composer of this generation deserves special mention: Jørgen Bentzon (1897–1951). A fresher talent than that of Weis, Bentzon's craftsmanship and his frank vein of lyricism are welcome. His music is civilized and his *Racconti* show a strong musical instinct allied with a skilled technique. His partsongs show an unpretentious but poetic gift and his delightful *En Romersk Fortaelling* (*A Roman Story*), though betraying its debt to his teacher, Nielsen, has a refreshing lyrical style. His talent seems to me of a more vital order than that of many of his contemporaries who sought stimulus from France, Svend-Erik Tarp for instance or even Riisager himself.

The most commanding figure in the next generation is undoubtedly Vagn Holmboe (b. 1909) whose achievement is as solid as his musical language is consistent. Holmboe was a pupil of Jeppessen and thus stems directly from the Nielsen tradition. After this he studied in Berlin with Ernst Toch and spent some time in Rumania collecting folk music. Much has been made of the relationship his early music bears with Nielsen and of his early fascination with Bartók. The *Symphony No. 5* (1944) has roots in very much the same soil as do the Nielsen symphonies and breathes much the same invigorating air. It evinces a nervous vitality and sense of momentum that leave no doubt about the vigour of his symphonic instincts. One is reminded of Nielsen in the slow movement by the quality of the woodwind writing, but too much should not be made of this. In general his wind writing is more austere thann Nielsen's, and as early as the opening movement of the fine *Notturno* for wind (1940) we find a distinctive voice, echoing perhaps some of the searching cries in the prelude to the *Theme and Variations* of the Nielsen wind quintet but nonetheless doing so in an independent way. After the *Symphony No. 6* (1947) few overtones of this heritage survive; the luminous, radiant woodwind writing in the *Symphony No. 7* (1950) and the *Chamber Symphony No. 1* (1951) inhabits a world that is entirely its own. As potent an influence is the neoclassic movement: Holmboe absorbed into his bloodstream the musical thinking of Stravinsky, Hindemith and the composers that they in their turn inspired like Tansman, Willy Burkhard and Toch. These sympathies find him in the main current of his time: his is no insular outlook any more than is that of his younger contemporary, Niels Viggo Bentzon. Undoubtedly Holmboe was drawn to Bartók because he also recognized the compelling fascination and inspiration of folk art. And his early achievement is not only the power of digesting various diverse stimuli, but also the assimilation of the folk music with which he came into contact during the thirties into the very roots of his highly personal melodic language. Obviously this language has expanded and deepened over the years: the personality we encounter in, say, the theme and variations movement of the *Chamber Concerto No. 8*, the *Double Concerto*, Opus 39 or the *Eleventh for trumpet*, Opus 44 does not call on the same dimension of experience as does the seventh symphony or the *Epitaph for Orchestra.*

Holmboe does not make big emotional gestures: his world of feeling is as disciplined as the expressive means he chooses. In the finest of his symphonies and quartets one is left with the overwhelming feeling that the musical processes that take place are inevitable steps in the working out of a drama. In a way the experience is not unlike a journey; the sense of forward movement is inexorable, the feeling of purpose firm, yet the wealth of detail *en route* renders it unpredictable. The symphonies composed during the late forties and early fifties have been written of elsewhere and on any single level their achievement seems to me formidable. Whether you set greater store by the degree and subtlety of thematic metamorphosis or feel that the secret of symphonic thinking is what Hans Keller calls 'the large-scale integration of contrasts', contrasts which will on closer scrutiny reveal unifying factors, or whether you feel that the hallmark of a symphony is its growth by 'the interpenetrative activity of all its constituent elements' (tonality, rhythm, melody and so on) the success of the *Symphony No. 7*, or its two successors for that matter, seems to me incontrovertible. Irrespective of their proportion the music grows consistently from the initial germ material which, in the case of the *Chamber Symphony No. 1* (1950) may seem relatively undistinguished, but because of the enormously resourceful and imaginative treatment that this opening idea and ensuing motives receive in ever-changing contexts, it acquires a variety of emphasis and significance that one would never have suspected. There does not seem to me to be one excess note in this work. As in all his finest pieces, the seventh symphony, the third quartet and many later works, there is a unity of means and ends so that the listener is never made conscious of the way in which Holmboe is fashioning his material. Its atmosphere is subtle and haunting and the more it penetrates the listener the greater its fascination.

The immediate impression that most of Holmboe's best music makes is of clarity and distinction of mind, while his orchestration is of a comparable translucence. The lines are for the most part clean-edged, the textures carefully, though never self-consciously, balanced and the overall sound picture is beautifully judged. Whether in the dark, brooding polyphony of the sixth symphony, the rarefied pale colourings of the *Chamber Symphony No. 1*, or the mercurial, luminous quicker sections of the seventh symphony, the scoring is always distinctive but never so brilliant that it distracts attention from the substance of the musical argument. Whether in the seventh symphony or the more recent music like the *Nietzsche Requiem* and the ninth symphony (1968) the sound world is entirely his own. Indeed in later years his scoring has, if anything, grown more luminous and more economical.

The sixth, seventh and eighth symphonies encompass a relatively short period of time (1947–52) and in the fifteen or so years that separate the eighth and ninth, Holmboe has not abandoned the orchestral canvas. The *Epitaph for Orchestra* (1956), though not fully symphonic in scale, is certainly symphonic in outlook. Its degree of organic integration and subtlety of motivic organization seem to me to match if not outstrip that of the eighth symphony and it is only in the breadth of canvas and the organization and integration of contrasts that it falls short of being a full-scale symphonic experience. *Epitaph* was one of a number of works commissioned by the BBC from various composers to mark the tenth anniversary of the foundation of the Third Programme. Like *In Memoriam,* written shortly before it, its concern with the tritone almost suggests a further working-out of issues that underlie the eighth symphony. Metamorphosis, about which Holmboe has written, is the very stuff of symphonic writing and indeed all organic musical thinking. Its most subtle example in the present century is undoubtedly the seventh symphony of Sibelius.

The string quartets are, however, regarded by many musicians as the centrepiece of Holmboe's output. In a sense they do enshrine some of his most characteristic and concentrated thinking and they span the greater part of his mature creative career. Apart from a brief gap in the late fifties, his cycle of ten quartets has unfolded with great regularity. Having discovered the medium, as it were, in 1949 (an earlier essay was discarded) he has never abandoned it.

The *Quartet No. 1* presents from the very outset an integrity that is the hallmark of the cycle; there is an organic cohesion, a completeness of statement so that one feels the composer has exposed all the relevant facets of his material. Its lyricism has a muted quality though there is a gentle hint of its fervour in the second movement. There is a controlled, inward quality at the opening of this movement, a withdrawn, slightly veiled melancholy against which a graceful but strange dance-like figure is drawn. Two other quartets followed immediately afterwards, both in 1949: in *No. 2* we find a frank, spontaneous and easy-going lyricism coming to the surface but it is in *No. 3* that one finds the most total concentration of ideas and feeling. One of Holmboe's most characteristic figures of speech is the device of exploiting tension between the major and minor forms of the triad, the harmonic structure upholding one form while the melodic line pursues the other. Examples of this abound in the quartets and it is also used to powerful effect in the closing bars of the seventh symphony. Some of the astringent flavouring of his music is directly attributable to this. The third quartet has great purity of language; all its elements are familiar – the dotted rhythms, the angular melodic leaps and modal contours and many other habits of speech that we encounter in his music – yet the total impression is new, an experience distilled and concentrated. The centre of gravity of the quartet is its finely-wrought and powerful middle movement, a chaconne, which single-mindedly explores one mood. The *Quartet No. 4* (1953–54), written between the eighth symphony and *In Memoriam* and *Epitaph*, is more overtly passionate. It represents to my mind a kind of watershed in the cycle as a whole; it opens a new world from which there was no turning back. The world of feeling it unlocks seems more complex and the areas of experience new. Its successor written immediately after (1954–55) carries this a step further: it is driven by a sense of purpose that strikes a more certain path than its immediate predecessor and the closing pages have a depth of feeling that call to mind the closing pages of a parallel work, *In Memoriam.*

The remaining quartets all come from the sixties. *No. 6* (1961) consolidates the ground won by its predecessor and in its subtlety in transforming ideas shows all the sophistication and skill of his metamorphosis technique. Yet in terms of spontaneity of utterance and memorability of ideas it is outstripped, I think, by *No. 7* (1964) and *No. 8* (1965). Both speak in familiar accents, yet in a language with more complex overtones. At times the seventh appears to be casting a backward glance, as it were, at earlier experiences and some of the devices it employs recall the first and third quartets. Both here and in *No. 8*, to which it is related in feeling, there is greater concentration and density of incident. *No. 9* (1967) and *No. 10* (1969) show his continuing concern with evolving an even greater control over his expressive language and with imposing a discipline on the finished work of art that springs from its inner needs. Holmboe is a composer who has developed, as it were, from *within*; he has shown an uncompromising integrity in resisting the ephemeral changes of fashion that have unbalanced so many lesser composers in the post-war years. He has never hung breathlessly on Continental trends and has never succumbed to the temptation to act as a kind of cultural barometer registering influences from without. His music, unfashionably, does not offer a series of aural diversions or discursive episodes; it has a continuity of thought rare at the present time and the quartets as a cycle are probably the most impressive of their kind, second only to the twelve Shostakovich quartets.

Holmboe's choral music is impressive too. Like Rosenberg or his younger countryman, Bernhard Lewkovitch, he can write naturally and effectively for the human voice. The *Nietszche Requiem* (1963) shows how resourcefully he could treat voices on a large scale, while at the other end of the spectrum one has little pieces like the beautifully-wrought *Lagerkvist* settings or the exhilarating and inventive *Inuit.*

Writing of the later Holmboe symphonies Wallner speaks of a note of 'moral elevation in the musical expression' and this is a quality one feels in the finest of his choral pieces. It is only in his keyboard music that Holmboe's contribution to modern Danish music has been relatively meagre. Two of his contemporaries make up for this: Herman D. Koppel (b. 1908) and Niels Viggo Bentzon (b. 1919), both of them active as executants.

Koppel's sympathies are clearly neo-classic and his admiration for Nielsen, Stravinsky and Bartók is evident from his scores. He thinks most naturally in terms of the sonata design; the fashioning of his material and its treatment sometimes suggest Prokofiev. The rhythms are virile and motoric, the ideas well shaped and often memorable, and he readily resorts to the use of ostinati to get things going. He made his name with the *The Psalms of David* which appeared shortly after the war but he is at his most effective in his purely abstract music, the *Piano Quintet,* the fine *Cello Sonata* and his piano concertos and symphonies. The *Symphony No. 5* (1956) is a striking piece and extremely well laid out. Bentzon, on the other hand, is an outsize personality; he is even more prolific than Holmboe and his output is simply enormous. Hindemith made a considerable impact on his early music as he did on so many post-war Scandinavian composers. Yet Bentzon assimilated Hindemith as readily as Holmboe had Bartók and turned this material into something very much his own. Even in the *Sonata* for cor anglais and piano, Opus 74, Hindemithian textures are paler and the mood more reflective and poetic though this is one of the more obviously derivative works.

Hindemith was not of course the only influence. Bentzon was a champion of Schoenberg for a time and made records of some of his piano music; he even wrote a textbook on the twelve-note technique in 1950. Indeed as late as his *Propostae novae,* composed in the early sixties, one encounters traces of this fascination. His early keyboard music written in the forties tends to use neo-baroque titles like toccata, passacaglia or partita. Bentzon comes from a highly musical family; he is descended from a famous nineteenth-century Danish composer, J. P. E. Hartmann, and is a cousin of Jørgen Bentzon. The *Partita* (1945) was one of his first works to be heard in this country and its spare, diatonic harmonies and rather Stravinskian textures and rhythms are very characteristic of Bentzon's music of this period. There are times as in some of the *Traesnit* (*Woodcuts* Opus 65, 1950) where the writing is too heavily indebted to Stravinsky but for the most part, particularly in the finest of the piano sonatas, there are no problems of identity. The sonatas probably represent the finest keyboard music to come out of Scandinavia since Nielsen; they seem to set out where the late *Three Piano Pieces,* Opus 59 of Nielsen left off. The third sonata (1946–47) has tremendous intellectual vitality and concentration; in some ways the English listener is reminded of Tippett though the affinity seems one of temperament rather than keyboard layout. The musical process seems to arise spontaneously and yet its energies seem subjected to genuine discipline. A fourth sonata followed in 1949, the same year as the fourth symphony (*Metamorphoses*), a key work in his development. For Bentzon, 'metamorphosis is the form of our time' and this symphony contains music of striking imaginative power. The work, like much of Bentzon's best music, is full of character but its power resides largely in the quality rather than the density of incident, in its imaginative detail rather than its concentration. The transformation of ideas, though an essential ingredient in organic thinking and developed to its highest peak in Wagner and Sibelius, is not the only factor in the organization of a musical structure. The *Sonata No. 5* (1951) is another impressive work, compact and full of a purposeful and controlled vitality. At times, as in the seventh sonata, one is almost reminded of Prokofiev but he has an original ear for texture; the *Chamber Concerto* (1948) for eleven instruments, three of them pianos, bears witness to this fertility of invention. The same muscularity informs the *Sonata No. 7* (1959) in which there are traces of serial procedures even though the most is made of their tonal implications; its power and ebullience remind one more of Prokofiev than anyone else. Naturally in so vast an output there is some unevenness; like Holmboe, Bentzon can lapse into routine and in a work like *The Tempered Clavier,* Opus 157 (1964) his invention can be thin. But if his very facility presents dangers, at his best in the delightfully inventive and effervescent *Chamber Concerto* for eleven instruments or the fine *Symphonic Variations,* Opus 92, he must be numbered among the most formidable Scandinavian composers of our time. Other Danish composers of this generation must not be overlooked: Jørgen Jersild (b. 1913) is Gallic in sympathies; Poul Røvsing Olsen (b. 1922) studied with Nadia Boulanger and has fashioned a language that is both refined and evocative. His style has been enriched by his encounters with non-European music; he is an ethnomusicologist as well as composer and has collected music in both Greenland and the Arab world.

Bentzon's enthusiasm for Hindemith during the forties was a by no means isolated phenomenon. Other Scandinavian composers hastened to make up for the time lost during the war years and got to grips with Hindemith, Bartók, Stravinsky and Schoenberg whose works, though admired, had never made much of an impact on the general repertoire in the North before the war. In Sweden a group of young composers including Karl-Birger Blomdahl (1916–68) Sven-Erik Bäck (b. 1919) and Ingvar Lidholm (b. 1921) used to meet on Mondays so as to study their works as well as the theoretical writings of Hindemith and Leibowitz. In Finland a similar cosmopolitanism is reflected in the outlook of such diverse figures as Erik Bergman (b. 1911) and Joonas Kokkonen (b. 1920), though Finland and Norway were not so immediate in their response to European currents. Why was the Swedish school the pacemaker in this respect? Part of the explanation may simply lie in the fact that the three Swedes mentioned were all Rosenberg pupils and that the impatience of the younger generation with their elders is likely to be even greater when the tradition they represent stands for less than that represented by a major figure like Sibelius or Nielsen. Not that these young composers wholly escaped the influence of the great Scandinavians, but it was little more than token homage. Blomdahl's early music showed him responsive to Nielsen, Hindemith and Bartók, and yet by the time of the *Pastoral Suite* (1948) we find the inward-looking Bartókian slow movement having a singularly Swedish accent and an individual one to boot. There is a dark intensity about this music that runs through much of his work during the late forties and early fifties. The opening of the third symphony (*Facets,* 1950), his best-known and probably his best orchestral work, shows this poetic intensity at its most powerful. Blomdahl derives the material of the work from a twelve-note series whose tonal implications are made the most of, and the piece shows a sense of organic purpose as well as a brooding fantasy that is undeniably impressive. Various facets of the series emerge during the course of the work, which builds up a genuinely cumulative effect. Like the symphony, the *Chamber Concerto* for piano and wind (1953) shows a strong sense of atmosphere and stark colours, even if, as in so much of his output, one regrets the absence of a generous melodic invention. Two choral works caused quite a stir during the fifties: *I speglarnas sal* (*In the Hall of the Mirrors*), (1953), to a text by the Swedish poet, Erick Lindegren, and *Anabase* (1955) to the poem of St Jean Perse, but it was with his space opera, *Aniara,* that he caught the imagination of the Swedish public. It did however meet with little measure of public success in Hamburg or Edinburgh. 'I was not surprised', wrote Hans Keller, 'to learn after 24 hours that the rocket ship was off course. With music like that you can't expect to get anywhere let alone to Mars.'[2] Whatever its failings, there are moments of imaginative eloquence in this score and some effective choral writing. The use of electronic music is also effective but against this must be set the passages in which Blomdahl's invention falls to the level of general-purpose modernity and where it is difficult to detect any vital creative impulse. Throughout the fifties and in to the sixties Blomdahl turned more and more to serial principles of organization, even adopting, in *Spel för 8* (1962), a certain element of rhythmic serialization. Like Bäck and Lidholm, he has a well-developed sense of texture; both as a teacher and administrator, his was the most influential voice of the three in the Swedish musical scene.

Bäck is the least known of the group. He first attracted attention with his *Quartet No. 2* (1947), a quiet, sincere work, and has made a considerable reputation as a teacher. Like Knut Nystedt in Norway, he has written a good deal of choral music including a series of motets that he started in 1960, much of it of high quality. His opera *Tranfjädrarna* (*The Crane Feathers*, 1956) is much admired in Sweden for its purity of style and simplicity of effect. Again, like Nystedt, some of his music strikes the listener as anonymous though he is a highly skilled manipulator of sonorities and an effective choral composer. Lidholm has a fastidious aural imagination and in many respects a more refined sensibility than Blomdahl's. His *Toccata e Canto* (1944) rightly caused a stir on its first appearance and still makes a good impression. He is highly resourceful in his handling of the orchestra and his ballet *Rites* (1960) shows him to possess qualities of musical imagination allied to a vital sense of poetry. Had he been less responsive to the newest and most fashionable techniques in vogue on the Continent the impact of his personality might have been stronger, for his eclecticism is as much a problem for him as for, say, Rautavaara in Finland.

There is a host of other composers representing a wide diversity of styles and talent: Allan Pettersson (b. 1911) who was a pupil of Honegger and Leibowitz and whose outlook reflects his sympathy with Berg. He occupies a position a little 'outside' the groupings one can detect in Swedish musical life. Neither he nor Gunnar Bucht have made a name outside Sweden. In fact, apart from Hambraeus (b. 1928), a pioneer of electronic music and one of the first champions of such heroes of the avant-garde as Varèse, Boulez and Nono, and Bo Nilsson (b. 1938) the whizz-kid from North Sweden who enjoyed a brief vogue while still in his teens, younger Swedish composers remain relatively little known abroad.

Outsiders who lump all the Scandinavian countries together tend to imagine that the Danes or Norwegians are much better informed about Swedish or Finnish music than they are. Although there are sporadic attempts at inter-Nordic collaboration, the extent to which each national group pursues independent paths, insulated from its neighbour, is much greater than is generally realized. Certainly Norwegians hardly hear more Finnish music than we do, and it is unwise to presuppose that cultural and musical intercourse between the countries takes place at any except a superficial level. Sweden proved a powerful magnet for avant-garde Norwegian composers in the fifties but cross-currents are the exception rather than the rule. In Finland only the hardiest plant could survive in the huge shadow cast by Sibelius. Madetoja was not only a pupil but absorbed many of the imprints of the master; most Finnish composers sought to 'grow away' and look elsewhere for musical stimulus. But their very reaction is a positive assertion of the power of the Sibelian magnet and even as young a composer as Erkki Salmenhaara (b. 1936) finds its attractions irresistible, to judge from his *Symphony No. 2* (1963) and *Le bâteau ivre* (1965). Moreover Finland, like Denmark, does less than its neighbours to propagate its own music abroad. Uuno Klami (1900–60) is among the most prestigious names in Finnish music between the wars, but his work is difficult to get hold of and little is heard outside Finland itself. Klami became a pupil of Ravel and was Gallic in sympathies but his creative drive slackened in later life. Others like Nils-Erik Fougstedt sought refuge in twelve-note music. Perhaps the most spontaneous and natural musical gift belongs to Einar Englund (b. 1916) who has a Prokofievian exuberance and skill, but the three names to have drawn greatest attention to themselves are Erik Bergman (b. 1911), Joonas Kokkonen (b. 1921) and Einojuhani Rautavaara (b 1928).

Bergman studied with Vladimir Vogel and his style is eclectic and exploratory. His breakthrough in international terms came with his *Aubade* (1958) whose combination of serial technique together with highly developed feeling for colour and atmosphere produces some evocative effects. He is much fascinated by the Near and Middle East; indeed as Istanbul provided the inspiration for the *Aubade* so the Nile has inspired *Aton,* a choral work with elaborate speech effects. Bergman's stylistic path is perhaps more consistent than Rautavaara's whose *Requiem in Our Time* for wind and percussion, with its Stravinskian asperities, put him on the musical map when it gained an international award in the fifties. His musical language since then has ranged from Stravinsky to Berg and, after his third symphony to serialism and aleatoric technique. The *Quartet No. 3*, which has reached a wider public through the medium of the gramophone, shows him to possess considerable facility and craftsmanship though his personality is not as yet a very strong one. By far the most substantial figure is Kokkonen who occupies a central position in the Finnish composers of his generation. His work is distinguished by a genuine integrity and though his sound world is less immediately identifiable than, say, Holmboe's he reminds one of him in that he has followed his own star and resisted the temptation to take the temperature of the cultural scene and modify his style to meet it. His craftsmanship is solid and he has the capacity to think in symphonic terms; indeed it is as a composer of symphonies (there are four) and quartets that he is temperamentally equipped. His *Symphony No. 3* (1967) is both effectively laid out and powerful in atmosphere. There is a sense of nature as well as a continuity of thought and well imagined texture (at times it reminds one of the later symphonies of Benjamin Frankel). Although he does not possess a strong stylistic profile, his music has a seriousness of intention and an accomplishment that rewards attention.

In Norway the same generation as Blomdahl's in Sweden or Kokkonen's in Finland is represented by Knut Nystedt (b. 1915), Johan Kvandal (b 1919), Finn Arnestad and Finn Mortenssen (1915), and Egil Hovlund (b. 1922). Nystedt is undoubtedly the most considerable of the group, at least in terms of reputation. He is an accomplished craftsman and studied in American with Copland, as did Hovlund. He is best known in Norway for his dignified and often powerful choral music but he also has a number of well-wrought orchestral and instrumental works to his credit. *De syv insegl* (*The Seven Seals,* 1958–60) which draws on the same source of inspiration as did Rosenberg for his fourth symphony, shows a fertile imagination and a deft handling of colour. He has also written a number of string quartets but, well-wrought though they are, they do not reveal a strongly defined personality. Arnestad and Mortenssen have both responded to serial techniques, the former leaning towards a Bergian expressionism while the latter is a more thoroughgoing representative of the post-serialist movement. Both Hovlund and Kvandal, on the other hand, have their roots in the language of neo-classicism and have a vigorous diatonic melodic style. Kvandal's *Symphonic Epos,* Opus 21 (1962) is his best-known piece and is both imaginative and characterful. Indeed it is among the most vividly imagined and skilfully executed orchestral works in the Norwegian post-war repertoire.

The younger composers of the sixties fall outside the scope of my brief. While they are many in number and widely diverse in talent it is too early to say who are of ephemeral interest and who will stay the course. Writing near to the event, it is far more likely that a figure who offers 'talking points' for the mass media will loom larger than the composer of substance who places greater demands on the intellect. Manner is much more easily discussed than matter and the reputations of all too many of the younger Scandinavian composers rest on their reputations! Scandinavia is enormous in size: yet none of its countries has a population equal even to that of London alone and although it is not the only factor, density of population is important in that it serves to stimulate talent, provides a more demanding testing ground for ideas and creates a discriminating public and high standards of performance. At the risk of stating the obvious, it is far easier for the less gifted to make headway in a less competitive climate. Moreover the fear of appearing provincial, like that of being thought old-fashioned, is highly destructive to standards and it is a fear that has powerful resonances in these latitudes. No one is more *déraciné* (or ridiculous) than the artist who consciously apes an alien set of manners at the cost of his own identity; no one is more old-fashioned (or ridiculous) than yesterday's revolutionary desperately anxious to avoid being left behind; and no one is more dangerous to the artistic health of a society than the critic or administrator whose values are thus undermined, for the result, more often than not, is that these fears advance the cause of the ephemeral and the second-rate at the expense of the first-rate. Music criticism in general suffers from an outsize Beckmesser complex and the result is an undiscriminating acceptance of experiment, irrespective of its worth and even professional competence. At its extreme it even extends a permissive tolerance to phenomena whose declared intention is the destruction of art. Such a climate is far more destructive of talent than the blinkered pronouncements of older critics that discouraged the great masters of the nineteenth century. For in the post-Dada ethos that marked much of the sixties, the antics of 'composers' who did not (and possibly could not) compose, as well as those who actively abdicated their role, have been accorded as much and often more attention and esteem than those who have made some effort towards mastering their elementary craft.

The sixties have seen the younger Scandinavians searching, as have composers everywhere, for some kind of identity. All trends and tendencies, like Mao's thousand blossoms, are flowering, even though not all of the blooms are particularly fragrant. Some, like Hans Eklund and Jan Carlstedt in Sweden, work within the traditional language of Britten and Shostakovich. (Shostakovich has been an influence on some Finnish composers too and on the young Norwegian, Edvard Fliflet Braein, whose work showed real signs of promise in the fifties but whose star has since waned.) Others like the gifted Norwegian composer, Nordheim, or the Swede, Hambraeus, have turned to the electronic medium; others have followed every conceivable post-serialist trend. Two figures among them show talent of a real kind; Lars Johan Werle in Sweden and Per Nørgaard in Denmark, both of them in search of a new language. Nørgaard is in a sense as talented as any composer working in Scandinavia; his early works up to his best-known piece, *Constellations* for strings, show an imagination and musicianship of a high order, and it is sad that during the sixties his search for new means has led him down or rather up the trendy, well-trodden garden path. Some of his later piano music and the ballet, *Le Jeune Homme à marier* (1965) are as shallow and puerile as any now being written but in them one does sense a composer of talent trying to get out. The seventies will see whether he succeeds. Each generation reacts afresh to tradition and doubtless the young composers of the seventies will be as impatient of their predecessors as have the young men of 1960.

Appendix

Short biographies of some further British composers

David Bedford, b. 1937. Studied at the Royal Academy of Music with Berkeley and subsequently with Luigi Nono in Venice, and also at the Milan Electronic Studio. He has worked as a teacher since 1962 and has written a number of works specially for students. His music is predominantly vocal, including several settings of Kenneth Patchen, and mainly accompanied by small instrumental ensembles. His best known work is perhaps *Music for Albion Moonlight* (1965). One could call him an avant-garde romantic because of his subtle feeling for tone-colour: his *Two Poems for Chorus* (1963) contain some remarkable effects within a mainly *piano* dynamic range.

Gordon Crosse was born in 1937: his first mature music comes from his period of study at Oxford, where he got to know the music of the post-Webern avant-garde and also Maxwell Davies and Birtwhistle. He then studied with Petrassi in Rome, and his music acquired a more dramatic character. His style fuses diverse ingredients into a whole, as may be seen in his recent violin concerto: his other works include *Symphonies* for chamber orchestra (1964), *Changes*, written for the 1966 Three Choirs Festival, and two operas, *Purgatory* and *The Grace of Todd.* The principal influences on his style have been those of Britten, Webern and Maxwell Davies.

BENJAMIN FRANKEL, b. 1906. After an upbringing in jazz and popular music, became known in the late 1940s through a series of sensitively written string quartets and later a violin concerto. Followed these with several symphonies which combine twelve-note technique with romantic expressiveness. Now lives in Switzerland.

NICHOLAS MAW, b. 1935. Pupil of Lennox Berkeley, and also studied in Paris with Nadia Boulanger and Max Deutsch. Has assimilated modern techniques but uses them in a more traditional way than some of his contemporaries. Has chiefly been interested in vocal and dramatic music: his *Eight Chinese Lyrics* (1956) is a serial work, but in later works such as his *Scenes and Arias* for three women's voices and orchestra he combines serial and tonal techniques. His operas include *One Man Show* and *The Rising of The Moon*, the latter a successful comedy which was performed at Glyndebourne in 1970 and 1971.

WILFRID MELLERS, b. 1914. Writer on music and professor of music at York University. Has written numerous works which show great ingenuity and originality; both his writings and his music have had a stimulating effect on music in England.

BERNARD NAYLOR, b. 1907. Studied with Vaughan Williams, Holst and Ireland. Held conducting posts at Oxford and in Canada. Has written many choral works which show a new form of the English choral tradition.

BERNARD RANDS was born in Sheffield in 1935. He studied at the University of Wales and later with Dallapiccola, Boulez Maderna and Berio. From 1966–8 he held fellowships in the USA and he is now a member of the music faculty of the University of York. His works have been performed at many international festivals and he himself has worked in several electronic studios in different countries. His works are mainly instrumental, but include *Metalepsis 2* for voice and instruments and two vocal ballads. He has also written a good deal of educational music. His works show some influence of Berio, but his individuality lies in his exploration of the sound potentialities of the instruments and his use of different tone-colours in a novel and exciting way. His most recent work, *Mésalliance*, was commissioned by the BBC for a Round House Concert in 1972.

Robert Sherlaw Johnson was born in Sunderland in 1932. He studied at the Royal Academy in London and then in Paris, where he had lessons from Nadia Boulanger and Messiaen. Since then he has held teaching posts at Leeds, York and Oxford Universities. He is an excellent pianist, specialising in 20th century music. His works, intense in feeling if somewhat eclectic in style, show considerable poetic imagination and contain some unusual effects; they include two piano sonatas, *The Resurrection of Feng-Huang* for mixed chorus and a string quartet which won a Radcliffe Award in 1970.

Robert Simpson, b. 1921. Author of a book on Carl Nielsen and member of the BBC music staff. Has written three symphonies which make a new use of traditional elements and have been widely acclaimed.

Roger Smalley, b. 1943. Studied with Stockhausen and shows the influence of his recent music both in his piano works, for instance in *Missa Parodia* (which also shows his interest in sixteenth-century methods) and in works for electronic instruments, for the performance of which he has formed a group, Intermodulation, with three other players. His *Beat Music* for orchestra and electronic instruments was commissioned by the BBC for the 1971 Proms. He is an expert pianist and holds a music fellowship at King's College, Cambridge.

Bernard Stevens, b. 1916. Pupil of E. J. Dent and R. O. Morris; also somewhat influenced by Rubbra. His *Symphony of Liberation* won first prize in the *Daily Express* competition of 1946; his violin concerto is one of the most successful of his early works. Since then he has written a number of works in all forms. Professor of composition at the Royal College of Music.

JOHN TAVENER, b. 1944. Studied at the Royal Academy of Music with Lennox Berkeley. He first attracted attention with his cantata *The Whale*, a dramatic work which includes speakers, singers, tape and various means of amplification as well as the orchestra: it has a vivid and arresting style. He followed this with a *Celtic Requiem* mainly for children's voices and based on a single chord almost throughout. Other works include the choral work *In Alium* and *Three Sections from Eliot's Four Quartets* for voice and piano.

References

Chapter 2

1. Hubert Foss, *Vaughan Williams*, Harrap, 1950.

Chapter 6

1. Hans Moldenhauer, *The Death of Anton Webern*, Philosophical Library, 1961; Vision Press, 1962.

Chapter 9

1. Robert Simpson, *Ianus Geminus* in *Twentieth-Century Music: a Symposium*, ed. Rollo Myers, Calder, 1960.

Chapter 10

1. Robert Simpson, *Music in Scandinavia* in *Twentieth-Century Music* (see above).
2. *Music Review*, November 1960.

Bibliography

General

Howard Hartog (ed.), *European Music in the 20th Century*, Penguin, 1961.

Frank Howes, *The British Musical Renaissance*, Secker & Warburg, 1966.

P. H. Lang (ed.), *Contemporary Music in Europe*, Dent, 1966.

Murray Schafer, *British Composers in Interview*, Faber, 1963.

Chapter 1

Edward Elgar (ed. Percy M. Young), *A Future for English Music*, 1971–

Michael Kennedy, *Portrait of Elgar*, OUP, 1968.

Basil Maine, *Elgar, his Life and Works*, Bell, 1933.

Ian Parrott, *Elgar*, Dent, 1971.

Percy M. Young, *Letters of Edward Elgar and Other Writings*, Bles, 1956.

Sir Thomas Beecham, *A Mingled Chime*, Hutchinson, 1944.

Sir Thomas Beecham, *Frederick Delius*, Hutchinson, 1959.

Eric Fenby, *Delius as I Knew Him*, Bell, 1937; new ed. 1966.

Alan Jefferson, *Delius*, Dent, 1972.

Peter Warlock, *Delius*, Bodley Head, 1952.

Chapter 2

Ursula Vaughan Williams, *R.V.W.*, 1964.

Imogen Holst, *Gustav Holst*, OUP, 1938.

Chapter 3

Cecil Gray, *Peter Warlock*, Cape, 1934.

Frank Howes, *The Music of William Walton*, OUP, 1965.
Constant Lambert, *Music Ho!*, Faber, 1966.
Osbert Sitwell, *Laughter in the Next Room*, Macmillan, 1949.

Chapter 4

Ian Kemp (ed.), *Michael Tippett, A Symposium*, Faber, 1965.

Chapter 5

Ronald Duncan, *How to Make Enemies*, Hart-Davis, 1968.
Imogen Holst, *Britten*, Faber, 1966.
Percy M. Young, *Britten*, Benn, 1966.
Eric Walter White, *Benjamin Britten, His Life and Operas*, Faber, 1970.

Chapter 8

Sonorum	Speculum	27,	Amsterdam,	1966.
”	”	32	”	1967.
”	”	33	”	1967/8.
”	”	34	”	1968.
”	”	35	”	1968.

SCANDINAVIA

Abraham Gerald (ed.), *Sibelius, a symposium*, London, 1947.
Bengtsson, Ingmar (ed.), *Modern Nordisk Musik*, Stockholm, 1957.
Horton, John, *Scandinavian Music, a Short History*, London, 1963.
Lange, Kristian (with Arne Östvedt), *Norwegian Music: A Brief Survey*, London, 1958.
Layton, Robert, *Sibelius*, Dent, London, 1965.
Layton, Robert, *Holmboe and the later Scandinavians* (in *The Penguin Symphony*, Vol. II), London, 1967.
Myers, Rollo (ed.), *Twentieth Century Music*, London, 1960.
Simpson, Robert, *Nielsen*, London, 1952.
Wallner, Bo, *Vår tids musik i Norden*, Stockholm, 1968.

Index

Index

Index

Index